ADvice By John Boggs

ADvice By John Boggs

Common Sense Stories of Local Advertising and Sales

John Boggs

iUniverse, Inc.
New York   Bloomington

ADvice By John Boggs
Common Sense Stories of Local Advertising and Sales

iUniverse books may be ordered through booksellers or by contacting:

iUniverse
1663 Liberty Drive
Bloomington, IN 47403
www.iuniverse.com
1-800-Authors (1-800-288-4677)

ISBN: 978-1-4401-7523-7 (sc)
ISBN: 978-1-4401-7524-4 (ebook)

Printed in the United States of America

iUniverse rev. date: 11/19/2009

Table of Contents

Forward

John Boggs is first and foremost a sales guy. This is the rock upon which his distinguished career was built and why the advice contained within ADvice is well worth heeding. No advertising glitz here, just battle-tested and market-proven sales and advertising wisdom for those wanting to improve their sales batting average. John's zest for life and passion for sales/advertising will put a tear in your eye and a spring in your step. ADvice…read it and reap.

Brad Lindemann – in business for life
President/CEO - Ambassador Solutions

The *How's* and *Why's*

Having been in publishing most of my life, I know the value of advertising sales. A consumer magazine has two main revenue streams: circulation and advertising. And considering that many magazines are willing to sacrifice circulation revenue in favor of the more lucrative ad dollar, the art of selling is paramount to success.

Sure, you can learn selling techniques. And maybe you'll even have some natural talent. But lucky advertising salespeople – and advertisers themselves – are those who find a mentor, a personal coach who can help them understand not only the how but the why of advertising.

John Boggs is such a mentor.

With many decades of hands-on experience, John certainly knows the how of selling ads. But his unique talent is knowing the why – and being able to impart that knowledge to others. Like you. Like me.

I've had the privilege of working alongside John for several years, and thus had the opportunity to see him in action. Both as an ad salesman par excellence and as a unique mentor to salespeople and clients. Yes, I watched him train people to be sure, but more importantly I've seen him motivate them.

Much of his knowledge, experience, and insights he has synthesized into an ongoing e-newsletter. ADvice (as it is titled) has been a guide, a manual, a resource, and an inspiration to those who enjoy an online subscription.

Now, with this volume, you have more than three score of his best sales messages in your hands.

From "What Makes Advertising Work" to "Who Are You Selling To," from "Back to Fundamentals" to "Lessons Learned," John Boggs will take you on an incredible salesman's journey. You'll get to know John. Also, you'll come to have a better understanding of advertising – both the how and why.

And along the way you will discover that you have found a mentor.

Shirrel Rhoades - Shirrel has held senior positions with Reader's Digest, Ladies' Home Journal, Scholastic, and Saturday Evening Post, among others. He taught Magazine Management for 17 years at New York University's Center for Publishing. Today he consults for companies such as DRG, Harvard Health Newsletters, and Time-Warner. He is also co-author of the textbook "Magazines: A Complete Guide to the Industry."

Will Google Going to Kill Advertising Sales?

I've learned in 30 years in business, by studying others, and by experience, that the answers we seek are usually all around us to see or hear, but because we don't know what we are looking for, we often don't understand them.

There is great hand wringing and gnashing of teeth in the media business because of the fear that new forms of media are killing the venerable and highly valued original content publishers. It is observed that the automated advertising methods developed to monetize the attention captured by search engines, social networks, and other advertising supported services seems to be flowing to aggregators, while starving original content. Google's system is so slick, just click in, enter your credit card, and buy some 'results only' advertising. Tens of thousands of businesses, of all sizes, have done so. Google seems to have built its success on the backs of the original content publishers while they starve.

Advertising networks have formed to distribute advertising from a single advertiser, via one 'buy' to many sites, promising to automatically optimize the advertising for the greatest return to the advertiser and threatening to move the advertisers' loyalty and the profits from the publisher to the math-magic provider of the 'results.' And now ad-exchanges are emerging offering the tantalizing prospect of "friction free commerce" on a "commodity" basis.

Advertisers like the idea that advertising can simply be bought on a commodity basis when they want it.

And sales people wonder if they are even needed when the world can so clearly quantify the results. How, they wonder, can they influence purchasing decisions if the inputs and outputs all go into a spreadsheet?

Interestingly enough, even Google has sales people! Actually Google has hundreds of sales people. And the Googleplex is spending millions of dollars on training those sales people to use solution selling techniques; skills traditionally associated with the most sophisticated sales needs.

Advertising sales is not going away. Why? For two reasons, advertising purchasing is a complex decision, and because although advertisers can purport to know and analyze results in great detail, results can never be known in advance. The so-called human factor enters into all advertising, and as a result, sales people will always – in our lifetime – be needed, and be effective, in the world of media sales.

But if advertisers can just buy their inventory through ad-exchanges, how will sales people fit in?

I suppose the answer to that is; the same way that wall-street sales people fit into Wall Street. Despite the fact that securities of all kinds are "traded" on exchanges and "market prices" sales people are some of the most highly compensated members of the big Wall Street firms.

So salespersonship matters. It matters now. And it will matter in 25 years. It matters whether you sell magazine advertising or TV, radio advertising or newspaper ads. And yes, Internet advertising too. That is why this book is needed.

Sales persuasion matters even in businesses characterized by exchange-set pricing. And it matters as much or more when qualitative issues come into play that can't be reflected easily in the valuation of commodity media. Train yourself and train your staff to prospect, qualify, persuade and close. Teach them techniques to engage the customer in a discussion of their marketing problems and needs, and to provide and configure solutions. If you do that you'll be acting like Google. And you and your media company will become more and more successful.

Daniel Ambrose - Managing Director, ambro.com, http://www.ambro.com

Author *Internet Sales Guidebook*; *Selling, Managing & Marketing Web 3.0 Media Brands.*

http://www.minonline.com/internetsalesguidebook_da.html

I found this compilation of stories, trends, and tidbits to be a welcome relief. As a long time publisher and ad director, you think you are all alone and your challenges are unique. NOT! Reading this book put things in perspective, gave me new insight on long running problems and even made me chuckle. John has wisdom and experience that even jaded know-it alls can learn from. Each chapter brings another ah ha moment and you find your head nodding in agreement but then the great reward is seeing how he solved the dilemma. I enjoyed the process of learning a new trick or two.

Marynell Christenson - Publisher
North American Media Group

David Ogilvy, considered the founder of modern advertising and his legendary firm Ogilvy & Mather, defined it this way: "Advertising is what you do when you can't go see somebody."

He is right, but that definition simply generates a multitude of questions for someone to wants to sell a product or service to someone else. When do you advertise? Where? How often? How much should you spend? How do you know if it's working?

Most of us don't have time to return to school to learn the answers to those questions. And I suspect all we'd learn in school is theory anyway, from professors who haven't had the bottom line responsibility to improve sales.

So the answer is John's book, ADvice. John has walked the walk and has taken the ivory-tower theory and merged it with real-world experience.

I publish a business newsletter, Creative Leisure News, and I've been reporting on the art-craft industry for 30 years. During that time I've seen thousands of small and large businesses go out of business, and hundreds or more make a fortune. Smart advertising is almost always a key to the success or failure.

Mike Hartnett - Creative Leisure News
www.clnonline.com

Acknowledgements

I really want to acknowledge the people in my life. Thanking them here, to me feels like giving an acceptance speech for something I have done. In fact what I really want to do is acknowledge who they are and what their contributions have meant to me.

First and foremost I want to acknowledge my wife who is my best friend, my biggest critic and covertly my biggest fan. I love her unconditionally and am surrounded by the glow her unwavering support. I also want to mention my children; Dr. Gina Evans, Julie Yee, Geoff Taylor and Christina Brown. Not only have they grown into loving and compassionate adults that make me very proud, they have also supported me through the tough times. My children have also given me the most precious gift in my life, my grandchildren – Kaitlyn Hicks, Leo Evans, Corinne Taylor, Damian Hicks, Zachary Evans, Cole Taylor, Jesse Brown and the twins, Emme and Elle Yee. I love them all and at one time or another each individually and as a group they have been the reason I go to work each day. I have carried in my pocket every day for the last 30 years, a rock worn smooth by my thumb and forefinger rubbing its surface during times of stress or uncertainty. This one singular stone is a symbol to me of the weapon that David used in slaying the Philistine, Goliath. Every day as I go out into the world to provide for my family I put this rock into my pocket to remind me of who I am, what I am fighting for and that I am not alone in my battle. Each of my grandchildren as they attain the age when they can understand, learn the story about grandpa's lucky rock and receive special rock of their own which I hope they carry even longer than I have carried mine.

I want to thank my dearest friend Charlie Slavik, who has played the role of my mentor, my boss, my partner, my employee but most importantly is one person outside of my family I would support unconditionally and without question. Charlie has been a fiercely loyal friend over our thirty plus year relationship. He has been a true friend in every definition of the word. He is the personification of that description of true friend who is not the friend who bails you out of jail but the friend sitting there beside you in the cell, saying, "Damn wasn't that fun." I have fulfilled a lot of requests for Charlie over the years as well as offered help and advice that was unsolicited and in many cases unexpected but I know the value of our relationship by knowing that I still owe him so much more than I have been able to give.

Thanks to all of the sales and media professionals that taught me so much: Bill Johnson at WNAP fm; Dick Yancey at Fairbanks Broadcasting; John Dille II and Ron Dykstra at Federated Media; John Robinson and Shirrel Rhoades in the publishing world. These and scores of others were instrumental in teaching some aspect of the marketing, advertising and the sales business.

Most of all, I want to thank the sales professionals that have worked for me over the years. Their energy, ambition, curiosity and drive led me on many adventures the result of which was a deeper understanding of the various aspects of doing business and serving our customers. Pam Satariano, Marilyn Covey, Steve Hartley, Mark Kolakowski, Jennifer Tandy, Gloria Bolden, John McDonald, Tamara Hanes, Jan Clemmons, Diane Kocal and Samson Lang are just a few of the obsessively disciplined and focused sales professionals I have been lucky enough to guide at one point or another during the development of their sales and advertising careers.

Introduction

Just before I embarked on a career in sales was I living alone in an apartment on the near north side of Bloomington, Indiana. I had recently left the employ of my father. After I left school, dad and I opened a small restaurant that I managed. Our business venture did not live up to our dream of opening several restaurants and the end of that relationship had gone badly. The lowest level in my life came one day as I sat inside my apartment and a knock sounded on the door. I could see that it was a young person professionally dressed who was trying to sell something. I hid in my apartment and did not answer the door for I was fearful of facing a stranger. Such was state of my ego and fragile self esteem as I was about to embark on a career in sales.

Still I needed a job and an income. So I answered an ad for a sales job at the local Ford New Car Dealership. There I met Tom O'Daniel, the dealer. Tom wanted to hire energetic and young, right out of school individuals to train them to become car salesmen. I fit the part and was hired with five others to go through a sales training program and a six month straight commission probationary employment. At the end two of the six of us would be rewarded with a salaried plus commission sales job.

During the training period, Tom spent time with each of us individually. He didn't have a specific training agenda he just filled what he thought we needed. I still remember the lesson on "spot" selling. There was a 1972 Maverick in the middle of the show room floor. It was red, with a basic 6 cylinder engine, rubber floor mats, black vinyl seat covers and 3 speed transmission. Other than the color it was as bland a car as you can imagine.

Tom took me by the arm and told me to begin selling at the left front fender. He said at the "spot" left front fender you sold; sealed beam headlamps, chrome bumpers and the paint process. Each product feature that you sold should include a brief but memorable story. I was told about the reliability of the sealed beam headlamp over replacement bulbs. The bumper story was the best because Tom told me the name of the guy on the assembly line that inspected every bumper before it was approved to place on the car. Finally, I learned how many coats of ultra finish paint it took to get the deep reed color on this particular car.

The next spot was the front of the car and under the hood where you sold the engine, the car's frame and suspension. At the passenger door you sold the rearview mirror, lines of the car from front to back. At the back of the car you opened the trunk and talked about storage space. The left rear quarter panel was where you filled the gasoline tank which was to perfect place to discuss fuel economy along with stories of the Ford engineers and the mileage advances Ford's test cars had achieved. Finally was the driver's side door. As you opened the door you pointed out features through out the interior. After you point out a few features, you put the customer into the car (with the new car smell), behind the wheel and you closed the door allowing them to be alone in a new car with the recent memory of all of the sales points you just made.

As Tom sat me in the driver's seat, I was ready to pay thousands for this stripped down car. For the first time in my life I understood what it meant to be sold something. I wanted this car. Even though my employment provided me with a free demonstrator to drive, I still wanted this car. More than anyone before and even since Tom O'Daniel taught me the value of telling a story to make a sale. Every story he told in conjunction with a basic feature, made that feature come alive and increase in its importance.

As I indicated at the beginning, my self esteem was very fragile and I was painfully shy when I was first hired to be a car salesman. Even I knew that I could never be successful selling anything as long as I was afraid to speak to strangers. I had to find a way to be assertive and bold in selling cars or I would never survive. But that just wasn't me. One day as I was thinking about this problem I hit upon an idea. If I could not be bold, who could be bold?

Beginning in 1968, there was a popular television show starring Robert Wagner that lasted for three seasons. It Takes a Thief was about cat burglar Alexander Mundy who being caught by the government was forced to use his skill on behalf of the government in order to remain out of jail. Robert Wagner as Alexander Mundy was the epitome of suave. He was cool under fire and never rattled. He was the perfect salesman.

So whenever I needed to be overcome my insecurity and fear, I became Alexander Mundy. I acted cool, suave and never rattle. And it worked. I became a very effective salesman in about a week, by just being someone else. This worked out so well that I added another actor's persona to my list. Burt Reynolds had just finished Deliverance about the time and his irreverent personality gave me the perfect devil may care attitude toward sales. Being able to "take it or leave it," as one of Burt Reynolds' characters added to my sales effectiveness.

At the end of the 6-month probationary period, I along with my alter egos was hired as one of the two full-time sales professionals at Tom O'Daniel Ford.

Over my many years in sales and the advertising business, I have met many famous people and many very great people who for some reason or the other were too busy helping others when the time for fame arrived. Each of them left me with a lesson or precious piece of information that molded me into much of who I am. After making sales presentations as Alexander Mundy so many times, it is hard to know what is me and what is not. But a good portion of who I am today was taught to me by others or assimilated as I imitated others.

This book is made up of some of the stories that taught me lessons about sales and advertising as well as the stories that I have used to help others to learn. There are no chapters as such, but a series of stories that have a lesson to be learned. I hope that many of you will highlight and mark the ones that teach you something.

Big fish, little fish

"I expect to pass through this world but once. Any good therefore that I can do, or any kindness that I can show to my fellow-creature, let me do it now. Let me not defer or neglect it, for I shall not pass this way again."

— Stephen Grellet

As I was growing up, I had grandiose plans for my life and career. I wanted to be a scientist, an astronaut and a doctor. I envisioned myself as being world famous. My grandfather was a wise man and enjoyed asking me what I was going to be when I grew up. More often than not, I would begin with the phrase "the top," "the number one," or "world famous."

Each time I shared my dream of which I would become, my perceptive grandfather would say," It is better to be a big fish in a small pond rather than a small fish in a big pond." He would explain to me that if I was important in a small domain, I would have more opportunity for achievement as well as create the possibility to move to bigger domains. Still, he didn't stifle my dreams.

As I grew and experienced the world, his words became more of a guide for me than I would have ever expected. I found myself attracted more to smaller companies where I assumed leadership roles and quickly made a difference. I was attracted to becoming a big fish in a small pond. As my achievements grew, bigger ponds (companies and opportunities) presented themselves. And so the cycle repeated.

What does this have to do with advertising? Everything! All advertisers, especially those smaller than Coca Cola and General

Motors, should heed my grandfather's advice. It is much better to be a big fish in a small pond rather than a small fish in a big pond.

How do you do this? Focus your advertising to a limited number of media options. Dominate the media options you choose and only expand to additional options after you become (and can maintain) being a big fish in that pond. How do you dominate? You grow and increase your ad size and even the number of ads per issue. Once you are the largest advertiser in your category, you dominate that medium.

Even the smallest circulation magazine has more readers than the average advertiser can accommodate. How many businesses could handle an influx of 30,000 or even just 10,000 new orders? Not many. It would truly be a case of too much of a good thing. Yet most advertisers focus on reaching as many people as possible with their sales message. Very few advertisers write excellent sales copy, so only a few of the millions reached actually respond. How distressing would it be if every reader in every magazine or every viewer of a television program decided they wanted to take advantage of your offer? No business could hire staff fast enough to fulfill orders promptly and still maintain good customer service.

Fortunately for all of us, advertising does not work that way. Consumers (including you) go through a very rigid decision process before making a purchase. AIDA is an acronym for this process. Awareness, Interest, Desire and Action are the steps each consumer needs to go through before buying any product.

Many of today's advertising salespeople are not schooled in how advertising works. Most do not know what it takes to be successful. Those who do often do not have the courage to tell an advertiser the price of success. That price involves steering the potential customer through AIDA: making them aware of your product, cultivating their interest, creating an intense desire to own the product, and giving them a strong incentive to act. As you can imagine, a ¼ page ad run twice will not in most cases take the consumer as far as you need them to go.

A competent advertising salesperson can tell you the truth about how much you should spend and what your expectations should be. Unfortunately, far too many will tell you what you want to hear: that you can get something for nothing.

There is so much more to effective advertising than the number of people you reach. Over the next several months, we will address some of the key leverage points under your control in the advertising process. Advertising is subject to factors outside your control – the economy, competition and timing, among others – that make flawless execution difficult. It's more of an art than a science. But if you apply basic scientific principles toward your advertising plan, as well as use common sense, much of the mystery dissolves.

A good advertising lesson to remember comes from the wisdom my grandfather shared with me, "It is better to be a big fish in a small pond rather than to be a small fish in a big pond."

Advertising results

"I have always believed that writing advertisements is the second most profitable form of writing. The first, of course, is ransom notes . . . ."

— Philip Dusenberry

It is so very difficult to convince some businesspeople to advertise. I suspect that a good number are jaded by their experiences with one of the many under-qualified salespeople that work and unfortunately survive in our industry. There are so many salespeople working in advertising that have limited knowledge of our business and how to make advertising work, that it leads to misinformation and disenchantment with the whole topic of advertising. Please do not get me wrong. There are great advertising salespeople out there, too, as well as thousands who, given the opportunity, will grow into outstanding salespeople.

Early in the relationship, a good advertising salesperson will educate you concerning the difference between responses and results. Knowing the difference will save you thousands and maybe even hundreds of thousands of dollars over the years. "I saw your ad" is a response. Your cash register ringing is a result. That is about as concise as I can put it. One appeals to your ego, and the other achieves that task of your ad budget.

Early in my career, while I was selling radio advertising, I learned how effective selling to someone's ego could be. I had advertisers who wrote and recorded their own commercials. I had advertisers who featured their sons, daughters, wives and employees in the advertising. Now understand there are great commercials featuring family and employees. But there are far too many of these commercials that are made only to satisfy someone's ego and/or to get that all-famous response of "I heard (saw) your commercial on the radio (TV, newspaper, billboard, etc.)." This type of ad gets great response within the featured spokesperson's circle of friends. Too often the responses are misinterpreted as results. Being patted on the back and acknowledged in this manner is very alluring. Unfortunately, acknowledgement of an advertising campaign is not the same as advertising results (sales). The number of businesspeople who insist on responses at the expense of results is almost as big a problem as the number of salespeople who do not know the difference.

I recently ran a company division that spent money on advertising. Over time our advertising campaign increased our sales with the targeted sector of business, but many of the division's employees doubted the virtue of the advertising expenditures because customers did not mention the ads (response). Now understand: The ads were not developed to generate feedback, only to position our product within the industry and generate sales (results). Since the sales were not discounted, i.e. tied to a "special," there was no connection to response. When I stopped running the division, the budget was cut and advertising was ceased. I am certain that ceasing the advertising will eventually end with lost sales from the targeted sector.

When businesspeople ask me how to judge their advertising expenditures, I tell them to look at their cash registers. Are they making more money since they have been advertising than they were making before they were advertising? To a person, they give me the oddest looks, as if to say, "Surely you don't expect me to make the connection between my advertising and my sales." I ask them why they advertise, and they say to increase sales. I then ask them why they would consider looking at any other measurement. But a lot of them still equate responses as being the same as results. The really scary part comes when I ask them if it would be okay if nobody mentioned their advertising as long as their sales increased. It still amazes me how many actually ask how they would know their advertising is working.

Faced with this mentality, maybe it is reasonable to understand why novice salespeople begin selling ego-satisfying programs rather than advertising that works. There are still far too many ads that feature family members and employees for all of the wrong reasons.

I learned the lesson very early in my radio career. I was not long out of school when I encountered new advertisers looking for response to their advertising. To solve my problem I asked several of my fraternity brothers to call selected new advertisers and ask for more information about what they heard in their radio commercials. It worked. None of my fraternity brothers spent money with the advertisers because of the ads, but my new advertisers were satisfied that their ads were working because they got "response." I have since found that focusing on results, although harder, leads to more stable advertisers and fewer budget cuts.

Advertising is a catalyst. It magnifies what is happening with your product. Advertising cannot and will not fix a bad product. It will not fix a poor marketing bridge. Advertising cannot make your product better than your competitor's product. Advertising may accelerate your success as well as your demise. If your product is bad, advertising will help more people discover it quicker. If you have customer-service issues, advertising will bring them to light much faster. But if you have a truly superior product, advertising will shorten the time it takes to gain market share from your competition.

There are many reasons to advertise. Increasing sales is by far the No. 1 reason. There are many others. Using employees in ads can be part of a campaign to increase company morale and empower your staff. Using relatives to do your ads may pay dividends beyond increasing sales. These tactics by themselves are not necessarily bad, but everyone needs to be very clear about what their goals for their advertising are. Responses are not results if increasing your sales is the primary goal of your ads. Just be clear about what you want and don't be sold something that feels good, but does not accomplish your goals.

What makes advertising work?

"Advertising is of the very essence of democracy. An election goes on every minute of the business day across the counters of hundreds of thousands of stores and shops where the customers state their preferences and determine which manufacturer and which product shall be the leader today, and which shall lead tomorrow."

— Bruce Barton

You have a great product. You want to let everyone know about the product so they will beat a path to your door. How do you do it? This question must be asked thousands of times every day in the minds of business owners that produce products. What is it that makes some advertising work and other advertising not work?

That's a big question. It is often much easier to find what doesn't work then it is to isolate what does.

Effective advertising is a combination of several factors. The measurements of reach, frequency and targeting the audience are critical. Then there is the combination of the message and the medium. Timing is important. And finally is the consideration of cost.

Let's get one thing out of the way right now. Money spent on advertising is only a cost when the advertising does not work. When advertising works the financial input must be seen as an investment. It is an investment because there is a return of positive sales revenue associated with the dollars spent. If you consider expenditures on advertising as a cost or as an expense change your thinking. Start viewing them as an investment. Once you do, your focus will shift to creating a positive return on your investment, rather than trying to reduce the expenditure. Reducing your budget will never grow your business. No company ever cut their way to prosperity. By shifting your focus to increasing your return on advertising investment, you stand a much better chance of growing your business.

If buyers of advertising, and those selling it as well, spent as much effort focused on creating a return as they currently spend on reducing costs, advertising would have a much better reputation. This is because more people would learn the mechanics of advertising, rather than relying on the mechanics of budgeting.

Here is one last word about cost. If you spend $1 and do not get the results you expect, it cost too much. But if you spend $10,000 and get what you expect, not only was your advertising a bargain, but you have put yourself in a position to make your company grow. Make sure that your goals and expectations are in balance with the money you are willing to invest. Nothing in the world is really free, nor are there many true bargains. When you end up spending less than you expect, you are probably going to get less than you expect.

But back to the question: what makes advertising work? Of all the factors listed above would suggest frequency as the most critical element in the mix. Yes, you must reach a sufficient number of the right people, and the message needs to be compelling. Of course the timing must be right. But in today's world people are so busy, they cannot consume everything that they see or hear just once.

In order to break through the clutter of the thousands of advertising messages each individual is subjected to, you must touch each person several times with the same message. Frequency is the most efficient way to make your advertising work.

National advertising studies show that the repetition or frequency of an advertising message adds exponentially to its effectiveness. Here's a good way to measure adequate frequency: about the time you begin to tire of the advertising message you created, people are actually beginning to notice what you are saying. Far too often, companies change their message before their intended audience is fully aware of what is being offered.

It is also good to remember how people learn, since you are essentially teaching potential customers about your company. People learn sequentially, from the most basic steps to the more complicated.

Put another way, you must learn your A-B-Cs before you can spell and you must learn to spell before writing sentences.

Good advertising allows the potential consumer to learn about your business. Your advertisements are the method you use to teach them. The better you perform in teaching your new consumers, the better results your advertising message will generate.

When you put it all together, your message must tell who you are, what you do, why the reader should own your product, and then ask the reader to buy your product. Of course, in all of this, you must teach your potential customer in the simplest of terms. And like teaching your child the A-B-Cs, you must repeat it over and over until they know it.

Each of us, if asked could easily teach a youngster how to count to ten, or learn the A-B-Cs or tie a shoe. It's a matter of breaking down the big picture into small easily remembered bits of information to be remembered and then repeating it until it is remembered. Why do most of us fail to realize how valuable this can be in growing our customer base?

We know successful advertisers are always cognizant that they are teaching new customers about their product. Each of their ads builds upon the last one. The really great advertisers are also relentless in using frequency to make sure they get as many of their potential customers to memorize their message as possible.

Measuring advertising

Henry Ford was credited with saying something akin to, "I know that half of the money I spend on advertising works; the problem is, I don't know which half it is." Measuring advertising is something everyone wants to know how to do. The trouble is that we try to apply simple solutions to a question that has many answers.

Let's discuss some basic business metrics before we get into ways to measure advertising. We are all in business to make a profit. You know, the amount of money left over at the end of the month, after you have collected on your sales and paid all your bills. Too often it is not as much as we would like or even what we expected. Everyone wants to increase profits. There are only two ways to do so. You either increase revenues (money in) or you reduce expenses (money out).

There are lots of ways to reduce expenses and frankly, it is the easiest way to increase profits in the short term. When expenses are reduced too much, however, it lowers capacity, robs you of reserves and eliminates the competitive advantages that enabled you to grow your business in the first place. As I said in the last chapter, nobody ever cut their way to success.

The other option is to increase revenues. Here again, there are only two basic ways to do so.

You can sell customers more. That is, increase the amount each of your customer's purchases. Remember not too many years ago, when you visited the golden arches, ordered your Big Mac, fry and Coke, and your server asked, "Do you want an apple or cherry turnover?" Ray Kroc's legacy for MacDonald's was creating one of the most reliable and efficient marketing machines the world had ever known. The server asked that question because a healthy percentage of those asked the question bought either an apple or cherry turnover. Those few words added up to millions of dollars in added profit each year for MacDonald's for many years. Selling just a little more to every customer, especially low-cost high-margin add-ons sales, create buckets of money on the bottom line.

There is just one other way to increase revenues. You can sell more customers. By expanding your customer base to include more people, you can increase your sales in proportion to your increase in customers assuming you are adding customers of similar value to those you currently serve.

Raise revenues = sell customers more or sell more customers.

But what is the value of a customer and how do you determine that value? Most of us know, or can find out, the total number of business transactions we have each day. We also know the dollar amount of sales we generate. We can even determine from sales records or by surveying customers how many times a customer visits our business in a year. If we divide daily revenues by daily transactions we get average transaction. Then if we discover how often each customer buys in a year, we can calculate the value of each customer.

Each day as I drive to work I stop at a little convenience store a few miles from my home. I buy a 24 ounce cup of Columbian coffee with a shot of caramel flavoring and foamed milk. It costs exactly $1 including tax. Not a big sale. But I stop there every day I am in town, which is about 200 days each year. Unfortunately, the clerks do not recognize my value, as they take my money and look at me as if I should be buying something else. It is too bad they don't ask me if I want a breakfast sandwich for another $2.50. Even if I said yes 10% of the time it could increase my value to them by 25% in selling me another high margin item.

Like the clerks in the example above, most businesses do not know or think about the annual value of each individual customer. Once you understand a customer's true value, it makes the cost of customer acquisition much more efficient. The owner of the store above actually does know the value of my business, as he buys my coffee and refuses to let me pay about once a month. Do you think I would consider stopping across the street for the $.95 coffee?

In order to effectively measure your advertising, you need accurate measurements of your business. You know how many dollars you generate each day. You know how many transactions you have each day. You can easily calculate your average transaction. It is vitally important to know the annual average value of each customer. You can survey your customers or use your database records to find out how many different customers make up your total transactions for the year. With these numbers, you can calculate the number of different customers you have.

You see, before you can measure advertising effectiveness, you need know what strategy you are going to employ. Are you selling customers more or are you selling more customers? There are a multitude of tactics to achieve results in both areas, but you need to define your goals before you begin to employ them.

By the way, when you calculate the annual value of your customer in addition to counting all of their repeat business, don't forget to include the referral business they bring you. Four of my friends now stop at the same convenience store each morning. I have told them that the owner is a nice guy and will occasionally buy their coffee. Two of them cannot leave without a couple hot, fresh donuts, which costs them an additional $1.50. Have you calculated my annual value to that convenience store yet?

Whether you are selling retail or wholesale, and whether our product is consumed daily or lasts for years, the value of each customer is so much more than the revenue you get from the first sale. At least, it is if you remember to think of the annual or (even better) the life time value of each customer.

Believe me, when you add up the $200 I spend at the convenience store in a year's time, the $400 spent by my coffee-drinking buddies, and the $1,000 spent by the donut addicts, and add it up over the next five, ten or 20 years, it adds up to $8,000, $16,000 or $32,000 in high margin sales. That potential is worth a free cup of java, every so often, to maintain the customer relationship.

Measuring advertising II

"There is a great deal of advertising that is much better than the product. When that happens, all that the good advertising will do is put you out of business faster."

— Jerry Della Famina

Drive three miles west, turn right at the first cross road then drive two miles north. Where are you? Precisely! It all depends on where you started. It is the same with measuring advertising. If you do not know where you are, you will have a hard time finding out what progress you have made.

In the last chapter of ADvice, we discussed the business metrics of average transaction, transaction counts and the value of a customer with regard to annual purchases and income from referrals.

Here's the secret to measuring advertising: are you doing better in terms of number of transactions (selling more customers) or better in terms of average transaction (selling customers more)? These are the only pure measures of advertising efficiency. Why? Any other measurement involves people, and the human condition is such that what they say and do is often too unpredictable for accurately measuring advertising results.

Early in my advertising career, I was selling radio advertising in a small market. One of my biggest clients was a furniture store. I convinced the store owner to use my radio station exclusively to advertise their New Year's Day sale. For the sake of measuring advertising effectiveness, we asked every shopper that day a series of questions. One of the questions was, "Where did you hear (notice the word hear) about this sale?" 65% of the shoppers said they read about it in the newspaper, 18% said they heard a radio ad on my competitor's radio station, 14% said the heard it on my radio station and 3% said they saw it on television, a medium the furniture store had never used in their advertising mix.

Advertising at its very best makes the customer aware of the product. Most customers don't remember nor care where they got the information. When asked, they will give the answer they think we want to hear. Or they give you an answer that sounds the most logical to them.

Direct marketing ads are those with mail-in coupons or toll-free numbers that often include a "special code" to get the pricing. Direct marketers use these codes to differentiate where advertising response comes from. This sounds like a great way to track the most effective sources of sales. But most customers do not respond the first time they see an ad. It usually takes three repetitions before the prospective customer is moved to action. Therefore, the third magazine/television commercial/radio commercial stands the best chance at getting the prospect to act. Does that mean that the first or second exposure was not important to the process? Of course not, but they were not given any credit by the direct marketer and will probably not be included in the next campaign, because it's only the ad that moved the prospect to action that gets the credit.

The true measures of advertising success are your basic business metrics. Know where you are in terms of customer transactions in both number of transactions and value of each transaction. Run your advertising campaign and watch to see what changes in your basic metrics. Are you having more transactions? This means you are selling more customers. Are you having the same number but higher value transactions? This means you are selling customers more. Are these results reflective of your strategy?

Another factor to consider is what happens when you change your media mix. If you advertise in a selected magazine for a period of time, you are servicing those readers. To walk away from that publication means you are no longer servicing those readers. The business they bring to you will eventually go away as your competitors continue to court your established customers. Your business metrics will change as time goes by.

What you do in terms of advertising has a cumulative effect. Eliminating one piece and adding a new piece may show sales dying off faster than you create new sales. You cannot expect new customers to be as valuable as older ones immediately, who have established a purchasing routine with your offers.

Advertising results are similar to a locomotive. You must shovel a lot of coal to get the engine moving. Once you are rolling along, maintaining the momentum does not take as much input. But if you quit, and the locomotive slows to a stop, it will take more than a maintenance amount of coal to get things going again.

My best advice is to monitor your sales metrics every day. Don't be upset by small daily fluctuations. Understand what they mean in the context of your industry. There is a natural ebb and flow to sales within every industry. There are seasonal sales cycles. You may want to employ strategies to raise the lows as well as strategies to extend the periods of increased sales.

Once you learn your business flow and its associated metrics, you will quickly see the impact of advertising changes on your base sales. You'll no longer be relying on inaccurate information.

Following the Plan

"In our factory, we make lipstick. In our Advertising, we sell hope."

— Charles Revson

I have writer's block. For the last week I have been tortured thinking about what I should share in this chapter of ADvice. The little voice in my head invalidates every idea, telling me it wasn't the right thing to say, advertisers won't be interested or it is not important enough.

Six months ago I decided to write this eNewsletter to share my insights and experiences in advertising with those who have less than my 27 years in this industry. Like many of you, I made a plan for the year and attacked it with zeal. After a few issues and some surprising compliments, I began to feel smug about what I was writing. Now, like many of you, the glow has worn off and it is beginning to be a little like work.

When things become work, we often lose our enthusiasm for it, and give it less than our best. It happens, not only with my eNewsletter, but with marketing and advertising plans, too. It is a time that can make or break your year. You can let everything slide and slip back into your comfort zone of doing what you used to do. Or you can push yourself forward, follow your plan to completion and achieve the goal you have set for yourself and your business.

One of my business mentors once told me that there is never a deficiency of great ideas but there is always a deficiency of great execution. The difference between outstanding success and mediocrity is more often execution than a great idea.

Do we develop grand plans and then let little pieces of them fall through the cracks, not completely develop or just decide it is too hard to do it all? Time and again, failure to fully execute a solid strategy is the biggest reason our plans do not work.

Advertising your business, like writing this newsletter, is not difficult. You are the expert on your company and products. There is nobody who knows them better than you. That is the problem. The more time we spend with our businesses, the more we focus on the daily routine and drop out those exciting facets that drew us to the business in the first place.

When I encounter someone just beginning a company, I thoroughly enjoy their enthusiasm. They are full of excitement and tell me all about their company in great detail. They will explain why their product or service is needed by the consumer, why they are the most qualified to provide it and why the consumer needs them. They have a dream that pulls them forward into creating a business.

Years later, these same people, even after experiencing success, talk in terms of product cost, increased competition, lack of consumer confidence and other negatives about their business. They have totally forgotten their dream of serving the consumer, making the best product, or being revolutionary in the industry. Some act as if they are a hostage to their own company.

It is human nature to forget our successes in life and dwell on the negatives. We love to share our pain with others. The process drags us down. These conversations create a feeling of resignation about the possibilities in our lives and businesses. And none of it is true.

Whenever I feel this way, I remember those new business people who are so excited about their future success. I think about those enthusiastic conversations where they share everything including the smallest details of their businesses. They infect others with their optimism in such a way as to guarantee their success. Each conversation with them is like a vitamin shot of optimism. It is addictive and leaves me envious wanting some of whatever it is they have.

This focus on their dream is what the day-to-day realities of running our companies, sometimes kills. We get diverted from the very reason we started our businesses to living with the complaints that crop up as our companies move forward.

Of course we are going to encounter problems. Any business without its share of adversity is not challenging the status quo. A business without challenges raises the question of whether there is a true market for its products or services. When we bought into our dream, the ups and downs were part of the package. We cannot be surprised nor become depressed when they suddenly appear. We all need to return to the dream and the excitement we felt as we shared it with our family, friends and colleagues. The problems, challenges, and – yes – even the boredom are all situations we must overcome on the road to success.

Others are more enrolled when you are building something than when you are tearing it down. You should always be building: building your business, building your career, and building something that others want. When you do, you won't lose your enthusiasm for your business – or writing a newsletter.

"Everybody knows me..."

"Doing business without advertising is like winking at a girl in the dark. You know what you are doing, but nobody else does."

— Stuart Henderson Britt

After nearly 30 years of selling advertising, I have heard every conceivable reason why some people refuse to advertise. Down deep, I believe most refuse because they do not know what they are doing and are afraid to admit the truth. So rather than ask for help, rely on an expert or show their ignorance, they fail to allow their business to realize its full potential.

Unfortunately, there are a small number of business people who believe in their hearts that there is no need to advertise. This number is always relatively small because, over time, a majority of these folks go out of business, only to be replaced by others with a similar mindset. Pointing out the high failure rate of businesses that refuse to advertise, seldom changes their minds. They are convinced that the ruthless rules of reality were written for everyone but them. To the very day they advertise their going out-of-business sale, they really see no need to promote their company.

Early in my career, I sold advertising for a radio station in a small southern Indiana market. One day, while calling on the owner of a children's clothing store, I had a very unusual encounter. He was the only person attending to customers so I was careful to make sure that I would politely step away if any customers came in. Not long after I began my presentation a young woman walked into the store. I stepped back and allowed the proprietor to ask the customer if he could help her. She said she wanted look around. The store owner came back and told me to continue. I gave him a couple of reasons why he should consider advertising with my radio station. He was polite, but as soon as he found an opening in my presentation, he raised his hand and said, "I really don't need to advertise, you see, everyone knows me and my business." Before, I could say a word the lady who was looking around spoke up. "I didn't know about your store. I've lived here for the last two years and I just discovered your store because I arrived early for a lunch with a friend across the street." Of course, her words were far more powerful than mine. She bought some children's clothes and he bought an advertising schedule.

Advertising is an important part of a basic business budget. Establishing a retail or trade business is far too expensive for anyone to leave to chance that the right customers will "discover" you. All too often, advertising is thought of as optional. It is typically the part of the budget that is often cut first. When business is slow, many people will reduce their advertising budget, when in fact advertising is one of the best alternatives available for increasing business activity and hence revenues.

Establishing an advertising budget is not easy. Spending too little is like throwing money away, but spending too much may seem wasteful. How much is enough? There are lots of opinions on how you establish an advertising budget. Many use a percentage of last year's gross sales. Others make it a percentage of the current year's forecasted sales, which make more sense to me. One thing is certain: servicing your established customer base, i.e. last year's business, is the least expensive part of the equation. Adding to, or expanding, the customer base by bringing in new buyers is a more expensive proposition. Why? Because your established customers know you and it is easier to get their repeat business. However, new business is more difficult and expensive to create. Still, we all must do both if we intend for our businesses to grow and make up for customer attrition.

When deciding how much to spend on your established business versus new business, the ratio that works best is 1 to 2 on a per customer basis. It generally costs twice as much for new customer acquisition than it does for customer maintenance. However, new customers are your true growth. So if, you are sincere about growing your business, you must spend dollars targeted on new business every year. You cannot afford to stop servicing your established customer base in the meantime. Your competitors will take those "loyal" customers as soon as you do. A growing company's advertising budget should increase every year. If yours does not, you are kidding yourself about growth.

I am painfully aware that many who read this chapter of ADvice will see the logic presented but never heed what is said. In the mid 1980's, after fulfilling many years of raising my younger brothers and me, my own mother opened a retail shoe store in her hometown. At that time, I was the general manager of a radio station in town about 150 miles away. I wanted to help my mother to be successful, plus she thinks I am the world's best and smartest son. But even that wasn't enough.

Over a series of telephone calls, I helped Mom establish a business budget, including an amount each month for advertising. I even arranged for one of my local on-air personalities to record a series of radio commercials for her business to run on her local radio station. A couple of days after she opened her store, I called to see how the business was doing. Mom said it was great. I asked how she liked the radio commercials. She loved them, but didn't need to use them since everybody in town "knew" her and came to the grand opening. I warned her that she needed to advertise to firmly get her business established. She said she would. The business went along well while the novelty of a new business lasted but eventually sales started to slide. I asked mom to begin advertising to increase sales. She said she would as soon as she got some extra money....

To make a long and painful story short, my mother finally did advertise. Her going out-of-business sale was the biggest success her shoe store had. Her dream of owning a retail store was ended by the fact that she failed advertise her business, thinking that good products and good service was enough to make her business successful. She refused to spend money on advertising when she had it and had to borrow against future sales in order to advertise to go out of business.

Take heed: advertising is not an option. There is a relationship between how much a company advertises and its sales revenues. We've discussed in previous chapters how to determine and monitor that relationship. For the many that will read and agree with this information, then hesitate to use it, I ask you to reconsider. For those who still believe that advertising is an option, I fear you may be doomed to the same ending in business as my own mother. But, what the heck! Mom didn't listen to me, either!

Sampling and demonstrations

"Advertising is the most fun you can have with your clothes on."

— Jerry Della Femina

I love to go grocery shopping on the weekends. Virtually every major grocery store has a legion of product sampling going on. I can try new brands of coffee, get a handful of snack crackers and sometimes get a waffle and sausage link. My wife has the authority to purchase groceries; I just go for the free meal.

Product sampling and live demonstrations are similar to test driving a new car. It's called the puppy-dog close. It all began with a pet store owner trying to sell a dog to a young couple. The couple couldn't decide if they wanted a dog or not. So the pet store owner said, "Just go ahead and take the puppy home tonight and in the morning if you don't want him, you can bring him back." Guess what happened? The couple fell in love with the dog and did not for a minute consider returning him to the pet store. Once you get a consumer to test your product, you've made a major step in closing the sale.

Why, then, do so many new and emerging companies fail to see the wisdom in passing out samples and doing demos? It does take some effort. Often it may take a special production run to create a sample of the product line. Distribution costs may be prohibitive. There are even those who think, "Why should I pay someone to give my product away?" If you happen to deal in a consumable product, it would do you well to mimic the strategy of drug dealers: give your product away in small doses until you get the customer hooked.

I assume that all of you produce fine products that are not in the business of conning consumers into a one-time sale. You have already learned to determine the lifetime value of a customer. It should be very easy to see the value of giving away free product or free product samples. But how do you do it?

Several magazines, including those I represent, can insert paper and non-paper product into the pages in our publications. We also can poly-bag our magazines and include "ride-along" products. There are USPS Regulations governing the costs, but still it is a fast and effective way to get your product into the hands of tens and even hundreds of thousands of prospects.

Another way is to offer free samples in your ads. Ask readers to call a toll free number or mail in a business reply card requesting a free sample. These leads can be handled by you or the retailer you serve in their area. Personally, I would reply with a coupon for the free sample and tell them which retailer where they can redeem it. This builds traffic for your all-important retail customer which they will greatly appreciate.

There are many other ways to get samples of your products into the hands of potential customers. Charity events, schools (My wife is a teacher. She and every other teacher I know would take every appropriate product sample they could get their hands on), libraries, nursing homes, hospitals, Girl Scout troops, 4-H clubs etc. The list could go on forever. The key is to make the presentation of your product sample appropriate to the distribution channel and always include information about how and where your product can be purchased. I would suggest including a coupon for a discounted purchase of your product.

Demonstrations remind me of the old carnival barker who has a booth at the corner of the carnival midway and who is shouting through a microphone, "It slices, it dices and it even makes julienne fries!" As a young boy I was fascinated by these showmen. They could make their product do almost anything. And I wanted to buy every one of them, even though I did not know how to cook. I was sure that I would take the time to learn if I owned one of those famous slicing machines.

Today, we are all scrambling for time. We want more and more in our lives, but have less time available for the things that are important. Any product that saves time, provides quality results, or offers us a small bit of convenience is worth its weight in gold. There is no better way to show those attributes than with an effective demonstration. Those demonstrations can also be used as the basis for an ad by showing before and after photos. Or show the materials and a finished product along with copy that is your updated version of the carnival barker's sales pitch.

In 1973, I was a salesperson for the Business Products Division of the 3M Company. We sold a relatively new product for small businesses, a facsimile machine. As much as I tried to describe what this machine could do, nobody could seem to understand it. After carting it into their office, I demonstrated how we could transfer an image from my Indianapolis office to their office by plugging the handset of their telephone into this large machine and making a call to our office. It was a monstrous piece of equipment, weighing nearly two hundred pounds and required a collapsible cart to transport. I absolutely hated the effort required to give these demonstrations.

After a demonstration with impressive results, however, many businessmen eagerly paid for the four-figure price tag. Today a much more compact version of the fax machine is being routinely replaced by email. Models have been integrated into most copiers. But those changes still don't compare with the remarkable transformation that took place in my customers' opinions after seeing that first demonstration.

We often assume that every consumer is aware of the innovations in our products. Certainly after we've seen them for a year or so, we forget the awe these innovations inspired in us when they were new. Demonstrations can spread that awe to customers every day, because many of our product features are always new to someone.

Remember that the media can help you deliver samples, or at least carry your product message to hundreds of thousands potential customers. 'Before and after' demonstrations and step-by-step illustrations can be shown in print and television ads. A person who sees they can make something of value with their own hands experiences a remarkable transformation. When your ad, product sample, or demonstration can give someone that feeling, you will have a customer. Without that opportunity for transformation, the customer will never try it. Give that feeling away with a product sample. When a customer has that feeling consistently, he/she will drive your business forward.

Is it worth doing?

"The trouble with us in America isn't that the poetry of life has turned to prose, but that it has turned to Advertising copy."

— Louis Kronenberger

On January 5, 2006, the CEO of the company where I worked, John Robinson, passed away from complications due to cancer. I lost a leader, a mentor and a friend. John was 60 years old. He shared his February birthday with me and another employee. Each year we'd be the first to wish each other a happy birthday. We shared something that we knew was special to only us. This year, I will miss John's phone call wishing me well on "our" day.

Losing someone close reminds us all of how fleeting life is and this confrontation with our own vulnerability tends to frighten many of us. When I first heard about John's illness, I remember asking myself what I would do if faced with similar condition. I promised myself that I would pay attention to those things in my life that were really important, my family and friends and the few things I believed in strongly. I vowed I would begin then and there to address the important things in my life. I would no longer allow my daily schedule of mundane activities to prevent me from living a life that reflects what is important to me. I know John Robinson did and I am sure that he made the right choice.

Without the presence of my own illness, I cherished those thoughts for a few minutes and then returned to a routine filled with a great deal of meaningless ritual that neither improved the world by my hand nor expressed my deep feelings for those who I love.

Henry David Thoreau said, "Most men live lives of quiet desperation and go to the grave with the song still in them." My biggest fear is, in the end, for this to be true about me. Yet I increasingly find myself captive to meaningless routines and rituals that are neither an expression of me, nor in my opinion, a benefit to mankind. I continue to live my 'practice' life. As if one day my 'real' life will show up and I will finally do all of those great and important things I am destined to accomplish on this earth.

The trouble is that we learn all too late that our 'practice' life is the only one we have. The 'some day' syndrome keeps us from being courageous every day and living life to its fullest. Even as I write this I am both inspired and apathetic about what I will do next with the little time I have left. I pray that I will not let my apathetic side win this battle.

Maybe I can inspire some of you to approach your advertising with a 'no tomorrow attitude' that will get you to finally "go for it." Some of us are not as excited about our own businesses as we used to be. Our daily habits have dimmed some of our enthusiasm to the place of boredom. It's time to look at our businesses with a renewed perspective of there are no tomorrows and today is the only day we have left to make a difference.

I often ask people about their businesses. After all these years, it amazes me how many will share a litany of negative responses. These people consciously chose to start a business. They are envied because of their courage and independence. They are the few the many wish they could be. They are 'big picture' people who have let themselves focus on the small daily annoyances of business, rather than the big advantages of doing what they choose to do for a living.

On rare occasions, I run into a person who addresses my inquiry with, "I'm living a dream. I cannot imagine doing anything I enjoy more than this, much less getting paid to do it." These folks are the ones who appreciate their own efforts. Their 'practice' life was when they were working for someone else. Now, they are in the game, living the life they want and being enriched by what they do.

Understand when I say 'working for someone else,' I do not mean in a business owned by someone else. I mean working toward the goals of someone else. That can happen if someone else owns the business or you do. The opposite of working for someone else does not imply selfishly working for your self. It means working toward an end that you feel strongly about and about which you are passionate. No matter who owns the business, when you own the goals, it makes a big difference. John Robinson was always passionate about his projects. His attitude was not to let what you cannot do keep you from doing what you can do. He extended this belief to include not letting those who believed you could not do it prevent you from doing what you knew you could do. When John believed, nobody could be more passionate. At his best, John enrolled many in his vision and we easily accomplished impressive goals together. But there were a few times when the vision was not as widely shared or was only owned by John. These occasions were painful because when he decided to do something, few could withstand his will and determination that 'this shall be.'

In February, I'll miss John's early morning conspiratorial phone call. Our birthday was one of his passions. A few of us in the company shared it and his passion made the day just a little more special for each of us. Even though he won't be calling, the day will remain special.

What type of company are you?

"Advertising is, actually, a simple phenomenon in terms of economics. It is merely a substitute for a personal sales force - an extension, if you will, of the merchant who cries aloud his wares."

— Rosser Reeves

We all try to define our companies and give meaning to what we and our employees do. I've worked for "communication" companies, "media" companies, "publishing" companies and a host of others in my career. Each one made their money from selling products or services. I don't think there are too many businesses who receive income any other way. But the most successful I've worked for defined themselves as sales companies. "Sales" is a word that conjures up images of a stereotype many consider unsavory and want to avoid.

In an earlier chapter of ADvice I wrote that there are only two ways to increase profits: you can cut costs or you can increase revenues. Increasing revenues is a sales function. Why is it, then, that everyone has such disdain for sales and selling? The health of our business and our livelihoods are directly related to the sales incomes of our enterprises. Yes, there are those images of the loud obnoxious boor at a cocktail party grabbing you by the lapel to convince you how he can insure your family's future after you die with a good life insurance policy. Then there is the used car salesman who is so slick in his approach that you instinctively put your hand on your pocket to make sure we are the only one touching our wallet.

In spite of our opinions about the selling profession, nothing happens until someone sells something. Factories would be idle without

28

orders, accountants would have nothing to count, and many others in non-sales positions would have no jobs without the activity generated by a sales order. The average salesperson generates revenues that pay the wages and overhead of six other people in their organization.

The most successful company I have ever worked for had two basic job descriptions: those who sell and those who better damn well support those who sell. It was really very simple. We were a sales organization, period. From the CEO down to the janitor, everyone knew their jobs were dependent upon the success of our sales staff. And every one in the company did all they could to insure the sales effort was a success. The esteem in which salespeople in this company were held was unmatched. And because of the manner, in which each salesperson was viewed, every one of them one took their responsibility seriously and sales revenues always excelled. When you expect the best out of people and hold them in high esteem, you almost always get what you expect. I cannot imagine anyone in that company having a negative view of salespeople.

What does all of this have to do with advertising? Isn't ADvice a book about advertising? Yes it is. Advertising has a major impact on sales. At the very least, it is an invitation for others to buy your products. So in a sense, advertising should be viewed as being just as vital as salespeople and your sales operation. The unfortunate perspective of many small businesses is that advertising is a luxury, sales people are a nuisance and money spent on either is a waste. Far from the truth, all of the above are a necessity.

When you regard your company a sales organization first and foremost, you see advertising and sales in a totally different perspective. Sure, you may have extensive manufacturing or service capabilities, but again the grist that runs that mill is money and money only comes after someone buys the product or the service your company provides. If all companies, including mine, considered themselves strictly a sales organization, our actions and strategies in business would finally be congruent with our financial goals.

Does this mean that manufacturing is not important? No, it means manufacturing is there to support the sales process by producing a product that customers want and desire in a timely manner that fits the customer's need, desires and budget. What about product development and research? With a company focus on actually selling customers the product being designed, how could these functions do anything but produce products that are guaranteed successes? In business we all need to work together. Viewing your company as a sales organization just maintains the focus of that effort on your ultimate goal, generating maximum sales revenues.

If sales revenues fuel our companies, then what is the easiest way to accelerate those revenues? The answer is more sales. What creates more sales? The answer here is putting more demand on the market through an increased sales effort or maximizing the efficiency of your sales effort through advertising.

When you throw a party, you send out invitations and then either call your guests to personally confirm their acceptance or request their RSVP. That is the same relationship between advertising and sales. Advertising informs and invites the customer to do business with you. Your sales operation completes the transaction for your company.

Your advertising effort should always have your sales goals in the forefront as well as understanding your customer's mindset and purchasing habits. If business is war, then advertising is your initial thrust, similar to an air strike. Your sales effort is akin to the infantry going in to take the territory. Working hand-in-hand advertising and sales make each other's tasks easier. The synergy of a well conceived advertising and sales strategy truly make one and one equal three.

So in your next public relations piece, please go ahead and tell the world that your company serves the needy consumers of the world. But inside the doors of your company make sure every employee knows that you are a sales organization first and last. Every action of every minute by every employee should do something to directly or indirectly move your sales machine forward or it is wasted.

And remember, all of your advertising messages should be designed to blatantly or subtly support the generation of sales revenues. Sometimes your ads can be emotive, creating a good feeling toward your product or company. Other times your ads can be a straightforward request to buy your product. But make no mistake about it, advertising and sales are about one thing: making your company more money. That's why you are a sales-driven company.

Who are you selling to?

"I've learned any fool can write a bad ad, but it takes a real genius to keep his hands off a good one."

— Leo Burnett

Knowing your market and its buying motivation is the key to effective advertising. Time and again I hear from disappointed advertisers the phrase, "Your magazine did not work." I always must hold my tongue, because I know that magazines will never work. All magazines can do is give the advertisers access to potential customers. It is not the magazine's job nor does it have the ability to sell other people's products.

Too many advertising salespeople focus on selling space or time. They do not give many advertisers the benefit of the thousands of hours each year that they spend looking at and analyzing advertising messages. All too often, advertisers focus on ad rates, ad location and magazine content. When it comes to the advertising message, they simply don't apply the same amount of focus or thought.

Years ago, when I was selling radio advertising, I handled the account of a national pizza chain through a large advertising agency. The agency devised a great campaign selling pizza for the family dining experience to 45-64 year old men. The radio, television and supporting print elements fit together nicely. The CEO of the pizza chain was a 48 year-old man at the time and the campaign played right to his heart. The agency won an award for their creative and media placement. That award still stands in the agency's trophy case at the entry to their offices.

Many men upon reaching the age of forty begin to have a more sensitive stomach. Often eating spicy foods in the evening leads to heartburn and indigestion. If you will notice antacid commercials, many use a forty-plus male as their spokesperson for this very reason. This is the why the advertising campaign did not increase sales for the pizza chain. As a matter of fact, since the pizza company focused solely on this audience and failed to promote to their core audience of 18-34 year-old adults, sales actually went down during the period. All because the agency failed to fully understand the pizza company's market. It was not that radio, television and supporting print vehicles failed to deliver the targeted consumer. It was that the wrong consumer was targeted.

I have seen ads where there is no "a call to action," asking the consumer to buy the product. I have seen ads where a strong call to action is present, but where and how to buy the product is absent. I have had dozens of advertisers cancel their advertising campaigns with my publications, saying that our magazine didn't work, when their ads did not ask customer to buy, and when they did ask, the ad did not tell the customer where the product was available.

Good copy is worth its weight in gold. Media can sell virtually anything when the advertiser knows his customer's habits and motivation, sells compatible product features and provides the customer an easy way to purchase within the context of this advertisement. The uncontrollable factors in advertising are then reduced to a dozen or so influences outside an advertiser's control, such as the economy, the general business climate, what the competition is doing, etc.

A well-written ad in a low circulation magazine will generate much higher results than a poorly-written ad in a high circulation magazine. Nothing can impact advertising effectiveness more than what you say. The second most important factor is how many times you say it. Finally, who you say it to, as in the case of our pizza company above.

How many times you repeat your message, is pretty important. The average consumer is faced with over seven thousand advertising impressions every day. Advertising is so prevalent that we are immune to much of its presence. In order to break through to the conscious level, when we've learned to close our minds to block out the sensory overload from so many ads, the advertiser needs to practice repetition in their advertising strategies. Every two to three years Coca Cola, Pepsi and others create new slogans. These slogans are in all of the hundreds of thousands and sometime millions of ads they run over the two-to three-year period. Why? They want every consumer to know and remember those slogans. Those very few words concisely tell consumers who the advertiser is. Shouldn't we as smaller advertisers learn the lesson of repetition from the big companies that are successful?

When your customer sees your ad once and your competitor's ad three times, who do you think is going to win? When you advertise once in a while, do you do so because you only expect to sell once in a while? If you want every day results, you must be out there selling your customer every day. Not only do you want to grow your business, but you must also defend the business you have won. If you don't protect your hard-won customers by telling them the story of your product again, your competition will take them away from you.

Find out why your customers buy and sell to those needs. Find out how they feel when your product fills their needs and sell to those emotions. Find out how to differentiate your product from all the rest and tell that story over and over. When you do, you won't be telling me or my colleagues that our mediums do not work. We've given you access to our audience and you have taken advantage of that opportunity. You have gained new customers and helped our mediums grow, because our readers, listeners and viewers love to be associated with savvy advertisers. They do want to buy products and services that fill their needs, but only from those who know how to speak to their needs and wants. Why shouldn't that be you?

Price, Quality & Service: Pick Two

"I would rather have a mind opened by wonder than one closed by belief."

— Gerry Spence

I believe it is time to review some concepts that I have mentioned before and look at them in a different way. There are some basic economic laws that are inescapable and that rule the business we do. In spite of the fact that some very intelligent people honestly believe otherwise, certain laws do control consumer and trade commerce. The first rule that everyone should remember is the most basic, but hardest to consistently believe: The value of a dollar is equal to one dollar. Yes—we are basically saying that one dollar equals one dollar. I really don't know how to say it any other way.

Now that we understand rule number one. This rule may shed some light on the fallacy that you can spend one dollar and get two-dollars worth of value. Certainly there are temporary minor fluctuations in the value of goods and services in respect to the market. But make no mistake about it; capitalism is a finely honed mechanism that does not allow for a margin of error of more than a percent or two over an extended period of time. It certainly will never allow a two-dollar product to be sold for one dollar over a period of time.

Our economy is remarkably complex and yet subtly reactive to changes in supply and demand. Witness the stock market's ups and downs in response to factors like the consumer price index, unemployment statistics, quarterly profit reports from major corporations, and even Martha Stewart's inside trading. With such a finely tuned economy, how can some people honestly believe that they can spend a dollar to purchase two dollars worth of goods or services? This could occur maybe once in a great while, but it would be unusual, and those times offset with an equal number of occurrences of spending too much for the same or similar products. Chances of overspending are about equal if those people making the purchases are not professional buyers. And, many who buy advertising are not professional media buyers.

The market dictates the value of products. Keen businesspeople adjust their pricing to capture their share of the market. But a $5,000 page of advertising that sells for $2,500 was never a $5,000 page of advertising in the first place. Come on folks. We are professionals. We make our living doing this. The only reason these stories exist is because some ego-driven people honestly believe they can get two dollars of value from one dollar spent. They want to brag about getting a discount, so they are convinced the $2,500 page they were sold was worth $5,000. Like I said earlier, maybe once in a great while you will encounter an honest bargain, but the true bargains usually go to those who spend lots of money and do so consistently. Why would any one of us give a great discount to a brand-new customer with no track record for payment, repeat advertising or fulfillment of our consumer's expectations? Those kinds of deals, although rare, are usually reserved for our long-standing customers. So if you as a new customer are offered an unbelievable deal, it is probably just that, unbelievable and nowhere near to the value you think you are getting.

Price, quality and service are the three basic measures we use to calculate product value. These three measures have an interesting relationship in a capitalist economy. It is only possible for two of the three to coexist with a certain product. Since price generates the revenue to pay for product quality and customer service, the equation mandates that to have both, quality and service the product must come with a hefty price. If you cut the price, you reduce investment into either product quality or customer service. This is a fact, not just my opinion. It is a basic economic law like the value of a dollar. It is also common sense.

Again, armed with this information you can make informed decisions. Knowing what you may be sacrificing in order to get a lower price allows you to work harder to compensate for less customer service, or to lower your product-quality expectations in the case of lesser materials. With honest expectations you can confidently spend a dollar and be happy with a dollar's worth of value on the terms you plan to receive.

Another law of economic certainty is the cost of what you want has nothing to do with what you are willing to spend. Let me restate that: What you have available to spend has nothing to do with the cost of what you want to buy. Case in point, I have $45,000 to spend on a nice automobile for myself, therefore a brand-new Mercedes 500SL should cost $45,000. Unfortunately, what I have or want to spend has nothing to do with the cost of what I want. Wise buyers suspend their opinion of what they are willing to spend until they discover what the marketplace determines the value of the product to be. Again, our supply and demand economy really doesn't allow a two-dollar product to sell for one dollar, except in rare instances. Fortunately for those of us who buy with our heart and not our mind, the marketplace also prevents a two-dollar product from being sold for $10. You may overpay a little, but seldom will the marketplace allow an informed buyer to pay more than a percent or two, premium.

And finally there is an inescapable truth about buying products and services. It is always better to spend ten percent more than the market says you should spend on a product or as service. Here's why: It is best to spend a little bit more for a product and be assured that it will do all you expect it to do. You then get all of the value you intend to purchase. You do not want to spend ten percent less than you expect and buy a product that does not fulfill your expectations. When you buy a product that does not fulfill your expectations, you, in essence, get nothing for the money you spent. So even though it is only 90 percent of your anticipated cost, all of the money is wasted.

The days of raising prices the week before a big sale, so you can then cut the higher prices, offering bigger discounts and still selling for a profit, are gone. Today's consumers are too smart for that ploy. Unfortunately in the advertising business, many companies still employ similar tactics when setting advertising rates. If they can afford to give you 50-percent discounts, what does that tell you about their published pricing? Paper-and-ink pricing seldom vary that much. The postal rates are pretty predictable. And nearly every publisher has controls on overhead costs. That being the case, how can you be sure that the next guy does not get a 55-percent discount?

Common sense should be applied to buying a business-to-business service such as advertising. If it sounds too good to be true, trust your instincts, it is. Either you were not getting the product you expected at the published price, or now, you are not getting what you expect for the discounted price. Beware of the great deal. The realities of economics make it impossible to consistently get great deals. No company can survive long term selling for a loss. And honestly, do you want to be advised by an employee of a company that cannot even profitably manage their own business?

Remember these rules because they are common sense. They will also help you sniff out an offer that is fishy. More importantly they will establish expectations in you that fit with long-term reality. That is important because we all do business in the real world with real money, and we want it to matter. So when you are promised the best quality available, with unmatched customer service at price lower than all the other products in the category, hold on to your wallet. You are about to be taken.

Basic Laws of Economics

"Many a small thing has been made large by the right kind of advertising."

— Mark Twain

How many of you would buy a ten dollar bill from me for five dollars? I am willing to bet every one of you would do so, if you knew that I would actually be foolish enough to sell ten dollar bills for one-half of their value. We all know that there are some basic economic laws and one of them says, "A dollar is worth a dollar, no more and no less."

Why is it then that so many advertisers believe they can purchase circulation numbers for less than the cost of printing and distributing a magazine? I continually hear stories from advertisers who swear they purchase ads in magazines that have 200,000, 300,000 or 400,000 copies in circulation, at prices that cannot even cover the cost of the paper and ink to print the page. Either these good people are lying to me or they are repeating the lies told to them. A dollar is only worth a dollar. You cannot get ten dollars worth of value for a single dollar. There are people far smarter than you and I who would have cornered the market on this if it were true.

It never fails to amaze me how the most reasonable and seemingly intelligent people can be convinced that they can consistently buy a product below cost. It is an economic impossibility for anything other than very special short-term circumstances. As a business person, none of us would want this practice to become commonplace. If it did, the laws of economic balance would require each of us to sell our products at a loss in order to compete. Our entire economic system would quickly drain itself and free enterprise, as we know it today, would end.

Why then do we continue to erode other companies' profits and yet are offended at the suggestion of doing so with our own?

There are two things wrong with advertising: how it is sold and how it is bought. When buyers focus on price, salespeople are tempted to inflate circulation numbers in order to lower the perceived cost. But basic laws of economics tell us that you cannot consistently buy a product at a loss. Yet the more price pressure is put on the market, the more temptation salespeople face to inflate the product value. Eventually, buyers are only dealing with lies and exaggerations. Does the biggest liar always win? We all know that businesses cannot continue to sell to us at a loss, but too many believe that they are the exception to this rule.

You get what you pay for. Advertising people seldom overcharge customers. There is too much competition to do so. The problem is too many advertisers actually believe they are getting more than they are. Their insistence on getting a deal leads weaker salespeople to promise more than they actually deliver. I know. I have called several competitors for rates and circulation, and then have checked their quoted circulation against their certified numbers.

So when you think you are getting a something too good to be true, I suspect you are only getting exactly what you are paying for in today's business environment, but you are being led to believe it is so much more. Paper, postal and newsstand promotional costs are all rising. No publisher can maintain the same circulation numbers as a few years ago without raising advertising rates. If advertising rates are not going up, then what you are buying is going down. It is an economic certainty.

The good news in all of this is that nobody in the craft industry actually needs an additional 400,000 customers. When you analyze your business and discover your market share, you may well discover you could not handle a business increase such as this. Remember, once you determine the annual value of your customer and divide your growth goal by this number, you arrive at the number of new customers needed to reach your increased sales goal. In the majority of cases, the number of new customers required to provide your sales growth will represent only a portion of the circulation available to any magazine in your category.

Relying on price to make your media buying decision is as dangerous as relying on price to decide which surgery you need when you have a failing heart. A tonsillectomy is much cheaper than triple bypass heart surgery, but when your life is at stake, you are not buying solely on price. As a matter of fact, I am willing to bet that if the price of heart surgery is not as high as you expect, you will be looking for a second opinion. You see, your life is very important and you want the make sure you pay enough to get well. You will even be willing to pay a little too much in order to make sure you get well. Yet too many advertisers are only willing to pay what they want to pay, but rarely willing to pay what is needed to pay, in order to grow their businesses.

Many never consider the content of their message or how targeted is their media buy. What you say and how you say it is as important as to whom you say it. I often tell the story of the $15 Cadillac. A very rich man bought a new Cadillac and in the first week decided he didn't like it. The dealership would not refund his money. They would only give him a "trade-in" value for a car less than a week old. In frustration he tried to sell this new Cadillac in a local newspaper ad for $15. The newspaper had a lot of readers. Yet nobody responded to the advertisement. The reason was that the offer was too good to be true. And because it seemed so unrealistic, nobody who read the ad bothered calling even though many of them were interested in buying a car. Your message must convey value for your product in balance with the price of your product. Our consuming public is far too wise to fall for bait and switch ads or other con jobs designed to fool them into acting. Again, a dollar is worth a dollar, as is the perception of a dollar.

When someone offers you a discount, you should ask yourself why. Nobody offers to cut their price without a solid reason. The only time I offer price concessions is for my convenience. When I want to increase the amount of booked revenue well in advance, when I want to increase my dominance in certain business categories, and sometimes when I am training sales people, I am likely to offer price breaks. I trade this profitability for other strategic advantages. Want a discount from me? Offer me a strategic marketplace advantage and you will win my heart. I never discount for someone else's convenience. Neither do my competitors. Be very wary of anyone who gives discounts because "they like you." Either you are not getting a true discount, or you were paying too much in the first place.

Remember, too, that by increasing the response to your current advertising, you will reap big sales rewards without any additional investment. Spending time improving and perfecting your sales message will give you bigger payoffs than shopping advertising rates. Doing so can literally double your sales. And I doubt if shopping rates can ever do that. Find an advertising representative who will invest their time and knowledge to help you create an ad that will work and you've spent your time very well. When the ad works well, differences in ad rates don't seem to matter nearly as much.

How to get good advertising rates

"Advertising may be described as the science of arresting the human intelligence long enough to get money from it."

— Stephen Butler Leacock

The pricing of advertising media has been made such a big part of what people consider in the advertising process, I feel I must spend some time talking about it. I really tire of these discussions because media pricing has very little to do with effective advertising. It is a necessary consideration but is so far off target that giving it more time than it deserves only perpetuates the myth that it is vital.

Advertising is, for the most part, a supply and demand business. There is a flexible but somewhat limited supply of advertising opportunities. Demand is determined by how many businesspeople would rather maintain the status quo than grow their businesses.

'Results' are the real capital of advertising. Unfortunately, only a very few take the time to actually master how to generate results from advertising. The rest are left to measure the cost of advertising as one of the common denominators they can understand to measure advertising.

Cost per thousand (CPM) is a measurement used to express the cost of reaching 1,000 people in an advertising campaign. CPM is a measurement developed by advertising agencies to simplify the process of purchasing different mediums. The task of calculating the CPM of various media options is left to media buyers. The position of media buyer is an entry level position in most advertising agencies. It is position where those without agency experience are put to learn the business and the development of this measurement alleviates the need for any advertising experience for those holding this position.

Measuring the cost of reach, i.e., the number of people exposed to an advertisement, is more accurate than measuring cost per thousand. Frequency is another advertising measurement, meaning the number of times the average person is exposed to the advertisement. The combination of these two measurements can begin to give you insight into the effectiveness of your advertising exposure. Exposure does still not equate directly to results. These measurements are often expressed in terms of their costs. The average media buyer has trouble calculating both true reach and true frequency. So you can see the need for CPM.

Reach and frequency against a target market point or one percent of the targeted demographic population in the measured geographic area is how major agencies buy markets. A strong advertising demographic is women who are 25-54 years old. Major market media will price themselves according to this formula in these specific negotiations. Not long ago, about forty-five cents of every advertising dollar was targeted at this popular demographic at a cost per point of about $65. In a large market with two to three million consumers, the total number of 25-54 year old women might be half a million. One point of this target audience equates to 5,000 women.

A campaign targeting this audience segment calling for 75 points with a 3.2 frequency means reaching seventy-five percent of all of the market's target demographic cell a minimum of 3.2 times with the advertising message. In the example above, this campaign would equate into reaching 375,000 women (75% of 500,000) an average of 3.2 times for a total of 1.2 million impressions at a cost of $78,000. When you consider that the measurement of television audiences, radio audiences, newspaper readership, complete magazine readership, outdoor advertising and online mediums are all calculated differently, it is easy to see why minimally trained media buyers ask for a CPM.

The big secret is that those of us in the media who determine advertising rates also know how to calculate these numbers. We also know that many of the buyers cannot do these calculations. Our pricing is seldom based on these criteria, because most buyers don't understand the calculations; those who do change the rules from one media buy to the next, in order to suit their needs.

Other than supply and demand, how do advertising mediums price their product? There is an arbitrary level of pricing that is set and fluctuates by demand for the product. We discount for our convenience. I repeat: we discount the pricing of our product to make our jobs easier. It would be easy to say that we set our pricing for the convenience of the advertiser, but that is not the truth. We may be concerned about your business trials and tribulations. We may be concerned about how much money you have in your budget. We may even care about how many gross rating points your media plan calls for. But we are mainly concerned with achieving our business goals in the most efficient manner possible and use discounted pricing and promotional pricing for that purpose alone.

We are in business, just like you. Every advertising medium has monthly revenue goals. We have bills to pay. Every printed page costs money. Studio time costs money. On-line designs cost money. We have employees to pay, along with their benefits. We take advantage of available technology to keep costs low. We must generate income to cover our expenses for materials, overhead and staffing. We'd like to have a little left over for the owners, too.

How can you save money on buying media? Take a moment to understand our perspective. We give discounts on long term commitments because it extends our booked revenue and allows us to plan more effectively. We offer larger discounts to those who spend larger amounts of money for the same reason. We offer discounts in order to help us reach our goals. Many times these opportunities come months before a closing. Most of us in the media are good enough at managing our revenue goals that we have achieved our goal several weeks prior to closing. We can then pick and choose which last minute offers from advertisers we accept and which ones we decline. Waiting until the last minute works more for us than it does for the advertiser. At the last minute, we often get good rates to sell off the least preferable placement. Yet, even the biggest agencies offer to buy remnant space or unused availabilities, doing their client a disservice.

Magazines do spend money for additional pages, so thinking we have no investment and would sell those pages for less money is very naive. Broadcast facilities (radio and television) are limited to the number of commercial minutes they can broadcast each hour. As they near those limits their rates actually go up.

There are times when true bargains are to be had. But they come much less often than most advertisers realize. Because too many advertising salespeople lead with "specials" and promotions, advertisers really have a hard time discerning which is a bargain is and which is a sales gimmick. When those true opportunities arise, you must be ready to make a quick and decisive decision. Those advertisers who complain the most about pricing are often the ones with least flexibility. And flexibility is a key to getting these rare opportunities.

As a rule, there are four things which will go far in getting the best advertising rates. First, buy early. The sooner an advertiser buys the better the chance for low rates as well as getting the best placement. Secondly, buy long term. The largest advertisers get the best rates. By making long term commitments, you maximize your budget to get those discounts reserved for the largest volume advertisers. Buying six one-third page ads at one time carries more clout than purchasing a full page ad every other month.

Next, be easy to work with by getting your ad materials and/or copy in early and in the proper format. If you routinely miss deadlines, causing the company to pay overtime to prepare you ad, you'll never be extended the lowest price. Finally, pay for your advertising on time, or, better yet, pay early. We in advertising know better than most the time-value of money. We automatically build it into our rate structure. Paying at ten days versus paying at ninety days saves us money. And we are willing to share that savings in terms of lower rates. This is the single biggest lever advertisers have in getting the best advertising rates, yet less than ten percent of advertisers take advantage of it.

The media knows that you have your own concerns in running your business. We do not expect you to learn our business. But by being aware that we have bills to pay, employees to care for, and have the same concerns as you enables you to understand why and anticipate when we are most like to extend our very best pricing.

The best advertising rates will do nothing for a poorly written or ill-conceived ad. A good advertising rate is no closer to generating advertising results than a nice hospital room is close to delivering successful brain surgery. But since almost everyone still believes that advertising rates matter, hopefully this chapter of ADvice has given you some ideas on how to extend your advertising budget.

How to get more from your advertising budget

"Advertising is the foot on the accelerator, the hand on the throttle, the spur on the flank that keeps our economy surging forward."

— Robert W. Sarnoff

One of the best sources you can have for market research and current trends is your advertising sales representative I know, many times advertising people are pushy. Some are not too subtle and others seem to be single-minded in their pursuit of closing sales. They always seem to be selling something.

But consider this: the average advertising salesperson speaks with thirty to fifty businesses per week. They consistently have conversations about where the industry's business has been, is currently and where it may be going. They know your business, your competitor's business and the business of those who are successful as well as those who are struggling. They spent more time in a week analyzing best advertising practices than you do in an entire year!

Some salespeople get by on their personality. For these few, their charming demeanor wins more sales than their knowledge. However, the majority of salespeople are hard working, knowledgeable, and in touch with current market research. In order to answer the vast arrange of advertisers' questions, they spend a large amount of time learning the industry, best advertising practices, and what the winners are doing that keeps them winning.

I generally expect those who sell to me to keep me informed of what is happening in the industry. My expectations are to be told about new trends, to be called when something happens that affects my business, and to be given the benefit of my salesperson's experience with companies similar to mine. In essence, I expect my salesperson to be on my staff but not on my payroll. I feel I deserve this service because I buy long term, advertise consistently and I am pretty much a trouble-free advertiser. Therefore, I expect to get added value from someone looking out for my business in ways that do not cost me anything.

Many advertisers fail to take full advantage of the information salespeople have to offer. And too often, salespeople fail to share vital market information that does not immediately lead to a sale. The typical salesperson/advertiser dynamic is one of selling and avoiding being sold. Because of this preoccupation by both sides, mental space for a meaningful exchange of market information usually does not exist.

My advice is to require each of your advertising representatives to keep you informed about the market. As a matter of fact, all things being equal, I would recommend that you advertise only with those companies who routinely supply you with such a service.

You must understand that ethics also apply to the information you should receive. My sales staff is aware that they are subject to immediate termination for revealing any confidential marketing information about any of their advertisers. The issue of ethics among salespeople is something that we all have a vested interest in. Advertisers need to restrain themselves from tempting salespeople to cross the line. Media managers must be very specific about acceptable and unacceptable behavior from salespeople in this area. And finally, salespeople need to practice restraint when they are the beneficiary of confidential information.

To share someone's advertising or marketing plan before it becomes public knowledge is the most serious violation of salespeople/client confidentiality. A good test is to ask yourself, "If this were my company's information, would I want to see it shared, possibly with a competitor?" If the answer is no, be very careful sharing anything with that salesperson.

When you find a good account manager you should find a way to work with them. A good salesperson from a medium or small circulation publication will do more for your business than a so-so salesperson from the largest circulation publication. As I have said throughout ADvice, a well written and targeted ad seen by a few will get more results than a poorly written ad seen by thousands. This truth extends to the service extended by a salesperson. Good marketing information used in a medium circulation publication will do more than poor information or no information used in a large circulation publication.

Good advertising salespeople are trained to help you grow your business. They can be a great resource if you use them. Many can tell you how much your business will grow through advertising, how long it will take, and how to track your growth so you know where the increases came from. Others can help you target your advertising message by surveying their audiences to determine preferences toward your products. Some can survey new products and advertising approaches as a form of test marketing. Very few can or will offer these services to "prospects." Almost all offer some type of value-added services to "customers."

As you negotiate your annual advertising buys, determine the various services available to your from your salesperson. As you leverage your annual budget, secure these services. Ask for more value when the media offers no further discounts. Find and use good market research.

Great media salespeople coach their clients in certain areas. Have ever noticed that in every field of human endeavor where performance counts, great coaching is integral to excellent performance, except in business. Too many of us refuse to accept advice or coaching from outsiders. The best coaches are no better than the ones they coach. But they do offer an objective perspective that is critical to success. Salespeople see the good, the bad, and the ugly nearly every day in your industry. Allow them to share or even coach you with the unique perspective that they can bring to you and your business. After all, you don't have to use their advice. But you might want to.

Finally, ask yourself a question I often ask when talking to advertisers. If you do not make and address daily plans for the growth of your business, who is going to do it for you? Few others in the world are committed to your success. There are few outside of your family who have a vested interest in this area. Your salesperson does have a vested interest, with the understanding that as your business grows, so will his.

Listening

"Nothing makes a woman more beautiful than the belief that she is beautiful."

— Sophia Loren

I love my wife. She is an extraordinary woman and is truly my best friend. There are times however, when we don't communicate completely. Because I know her so well, I admit I am often at fault of listening to no more than half of what she says. That's probably okay, because there are also times when, because I know her so well, she fully expects that I will understand more than what her words actually communicate. My mind-reading talents aside, you can see the perfect conditions exist for major misunderstandings.

In my day-to-day world, I often am too preoccupied with my own agenda to give her my undivided attention and listen to her concerns. When I get like this, she tolerates me for a while, but eventually, she takes me to task for my rudeness. Like many couples who have an established and trusting relationship, her method of restoring my consideration for her point of view lacks the diplomacy that my sometimes fragile ego appreciates. It's not really very pretty, but it is effective.

As I am hit with the stark reality of my lack of consideration, I mentally overcompensate and begin listening to her chiding with the rapt attention to the detail she demands, and that I used when we first met. I notice the wrinkle of her nose when she talks and the sparkle in her eye that forewarns of the passion in her words that are soon to follow. She forces her normally quiet voice to speak loudly to command my questionable attention. And even though she is upset with me, her ever-present smile appears in spite of herself. I am filled with the same awe that caused me to fall in love with her in the first place.

It is such a shame that I only really listen this attentively when I am gently, or not so gently, shaken out of my self-indulgent fog to really listen to what the most important person in my life has to say.

I have learned that listening, which most believe to be a passive activity, is quite the opposite. If fact, listening is much more active and engaging than talking. If you listen to the words, their meaning, how they are spoken and the passion of the person saying them, you will just begin to scratch the surface of real communication. Add body language, understanding the culture of the speaker, as well as timing and personal motivation, you might actually be closing in on the groundwork needed to begin understanding what the other person is trying to say. Most importantly we must suspend our personal interpretation of the facts and rely on what the speaker says to build a reference of his or her interpretation of the facts as he or she is attempting to convey them. It really is not easy.

Good listening evokes good speaking. When we pay attention to the conversation, it is like providing a highway on which the speaker uses his or her words to drive. Good listening makes speaking go much smoother.

The terrible truth of this knowledge is that it is wasted most often on complete strangers. For as human beings we feel we know those close to us well enough that we "know" what they are going to say, so we only give a portion of our attention to their communication and use our knowledge of them to fill in the blanks. For complete strangers, we listen to every word so we can build our knowledge base of them until we "know" them, too.

Salespeople, especially advertising salespeople are sometimes at fault of not completely communicating. I don't know how many times I have heard my sales staff say, "They know what I mean," or "I know what they want." Like my communication with my wife, conversations based upon assumptions or preconceived notions are breeding grounds for big problems.

Human beings have a tendency to be incomplete in their communication. We wrongly believe that others share our interpretations of facts. Because of this, most of us do not confirm if the people we are communicating with are coming to the conversation with the same basics as we have. Unfortunately the closer our relationship, the more this is apt to occur. In the words of my wife, "I do not need to tell you, you know me and what I am thinking." Certainly, this leads to interesting results in my family. The same mental process leads to problems at best and disasters at worst in a sales environment. Add to this dynamic the intangible nature of advertising, and it is amazing advertising people get it right as often as we do.

Is there a possibility that we as advertisers are not completely communicating with our customers? Do we assume we understand their point of reference for our product or service? Do we believe we "know" them? Do we only hear a portion of what they tell us and then "fill in the blanks," based upon what we know? How can we develop a routine of listening, really listening to our customers, and more importantly, to our prospects, and deliver what they are telling us they need?

Years ago in my broadcasting career, as I progressed from a sales manager to a general manager, I became responsible for programming. Since I had no history or experience on the programming side of the industry, I had little choice but to ask my radio-station listeners questions and rely on their answers for programming guidance. It was then I learned a very valuable lesson. Not only did I learn how to listen and rely on that feedback, but I discovered those peers of mine with a programming background did not listen. For the next four years, I beat them soundly and consistently in listener ratings. I asked my customers what they wanted and gave it to them. It was pretty simple. Those with programming experience "knew" what listeners wanted and did not want to be bothered by the difference between what they knew and what the listeners were telling them now.

Want to be inspired and excited about your business? Sit down with your customers and ask them a few questions and listen with every fiber of your being. Understand exactly what they are telling you, ask questions to make sure they know you are listening and to make sure you hear what they are saying. Dedicate time to do this so your attention is not diffused by something else you must do. I assure you that you will walk away from the experience renewed and excited again about what you do. Hearing the passion in another person's words is a miraculous thing.

If you want to get the biggest benefit from this chapter, go home and listen to your loved ones with all of your attention. Put the work you brought home aside, take the telephone off of the hook and listen to them. Watch them as they speak, look into their eyes and see them as they express themselves and honor you by sharing their thoughts and feelings. You'll fall in love all over again, just by listening.

Creating an additional market for your product

"'Be comfortable with who you are', reads the headline on the Hush Puppies poster. Are they mad? If people were comfortable with who they were, they'd never buy any products except the ones they needed, and then where would the advertising industry be?"

— Mark Edwards

Where does growth come from? When you have developed a market for your product and worked to get your fair share of that market, how do you grow? Do you continue to work like Coca-Cola, which spends tens of millions of dollars per year, to increase your market share by hundredths of a percentage point? Or do you employ another strategy? In the early 1900's the Gillette Razor company took advantage of market conditions and did just that.

Prior to 1910, the Gillette Razor Company had cornered the American shaving market with little room to grow their business. Gillette was even chosen to go to war with American soldiers in the Great War. During the duration of World War I, from 1914 through 1918, Gillette saw an opportunity as thousands of America GI's were in Europe and specifically France. American women were jealous of the stories they heard about the romantic French women. Fueled by the song "How you gonna keep 'em down on the farm, once they've seen Paree," Gillette ran an advertising campaign targeting these American women waiting for their soldiers to return from war. The message suggested that shaving their underarms and legs would make them more alluring for their returning sweethearts. Within a matter of a decade, Gillette had nearly doubled its sales and tied up this new market of selling razor blades to women, by creating a demand that previously didn't exist.

Creating a new market is not as hard as it seems. Before we talk about that, let me point out a key ingredient in the Gillette story above: emotion. Gillette played on a strong emotion in order to sell their product. Their strategy was not based on beating the competition's price, or even selling product features. They discovered a perceived problem, elaborated on it and offered their product as a solution. Too few ads from small companies strike at the emotional purchasing motives of consumers. Most think that price and product features are enough to create a new customer. Taking the time to develop an advertising strategy that solves problems with an emotional aspect will pay great dividends.

"When price is introduced before value is established, price becomes the controlling factor." These words are well worth memorizing. Any advertisement that leads with price, will contribute to a unique product being viewed as a commodity. Never make your product's price more important than the product's ability to provide solutions to real or perceived problems. Yes, lower pricing will stimulate sales, but those sales have lower profit margins and, even worse, they train consumers to buy more often during discounted pricing. Today's rush to "value-added" doesn't mean that you must sell for less. Quite the opposite, if you can effectively position your product as providing solutions to real or imagined problems, you are adding value to each transaction for the consumer without adding to your cost of sale.

New markets are not hard to find for those who keep their eyes open. My company, as an example determined one of our strengths was publishing project-based magazines for women. Two years ago we took those strengths to the predominately male category of woodworking and created the women's woodworking market. Recognizing that purchases of tools and supplies within this industry from women had grown from two percent to ten percent in the last five years, we were able to take that commonality (all were women) in order to unify them into a unique market. Those stores and manufacturers wishing to sell to this new consumer group have joined ranks with Woodworking for Women magazine to increase sales to a newly defined market segment.

In his book, The Roaring 2000's: Building the Wealth and Lifestyle You Desire in the Greatest Boom in History, Harry Dent explains the growth cycle of markets for emerging technologies and products. New inventions start off slowly. The first plain paper copier, personal computer, facsimile machine, portable telephone and other inventions were very expensive and only a few people purchased them. Initially all of these new products were considered unnecessary luxuries. As technology advanced, the price fell and consumer acceptance began to grow. Following a typical bell curve, new product acceptance didn't accelerate for the first few years and in some cases for the first ten to twenty years. But at a certain point, which equates to be about ten percent of the final market, growth compounds almost on a monthly basis. Companies that begin in new markets and weather the initial slow growth as the public begins to accept the product are the companies that make huge profits. Sometimes the windfalls come from being acquired by other giants in the industry, other times these companies become the giants themselves.

The point of what I've said above is that there are large rewards available to creating a new market. They generally do not come instantly. But they do come and very generously to those "overnight successes" who were the pioneers before others jumped on the bandwagon. Building new markets takes time and effort. The payoff, however, can be very rewarding

What are a few simple ways to create new markets? A store owner can develop a direct mail division that sells as much product through the mail as comes through the front door. Manufacturers can duplicate product lines and position one as premium-priced and the other as medium-priced, thus getting two slices of market share instead of just one. This is a strategy in which beer companies, soft drink manufacturers and tobacco companies are very strong. Companies can find secondary uses for their products and exploit a second market with virtually no product development costs at all, only marketing expense. Companies can find niches in their current market that they are under serving and become the dominate provider in that segment to increase overall market share.

To find a new market, you start by asking questions. Ask your media reps what they have that is new. Talk to reps from other publications to see if their audience is being served by your company. Think outside of the box about your product. Or, advertise those product uses that are not commonly known. Find a new problem that your product can solve. Above all, appeal to the emotions surrounding the problem. Human emotions are the most powerful motivator in the world. Forget price comparisons; most consumers are astute enough to do that on their own. Let your advertising explain why life will be made better by owning your product. Sell the sizzle and not the steak. But remember from our last ADvice, you must pay for growth. You cannot steal advertising resources from your existing business to grow a new segment, if you want to maintain your existing business. Basic laws of economics prevent you from getting something for nothing.

One final story about new markets is about General Foods. In 1934, General Foods began manufacturing and selling Jell-O. The product was initially promoted on radio and over the next fifty-four years the phrase, "there's always room for Jell-O," was pounded into of all of us. By 1988, General Foods discovered that Jell-O sales had flattened out. After hiring a research firm to interview hundreds of housewives about their uses of and views on Jell-O, they discovered that virtually every home in America had a box of Jell-O in the kitchen cabinet. The problem was how do to get housewives to use that box of Jell-O and buy more. A brilliant idea was born, Jell-O Jigglers. Not only was the Jigglers recipe aimed at kids who influence food purchases more than any other segment, but it also used twice as much product as regular Jell-O recipes. Finding another use for their product launched Jell-O into another sales plateau.

Finding new markets is exciting. Keep in mind the stories of Gillette and General Foods. There is not much that is more fun than seeing your business growing in new areas. You will not only build a stronger company, it will invigorate you.

What business are you in?

"Advertising nourishes the consuming power of men. It sets up before a man the goal of a better home, better clothing, better food for himself and his family. It spurs individual exertion and greater production."

— Sir Winston Churchill

According to Peter Drucker, one of the most important things an organization can do is to determine exactly what business it is in. This sounds relatively simple to do. It also sounds fairly simple to execute. But determining the organizing principle which underlies the products you offer to customers can be one of the most important steps you take in defining your enterprise.

A basic advertising axiom is to "sell the sizzle not the steak." We know that the customer is more apt to make a purchase in the glow of a perceived positive experience than to just buy a commodity cold. What motivates buying behavior is much more than a mere need-cost-value equation. Jan Carlson the former president of Scandinavian Airlines who was credited with the company's turnaround in the 1980's warns us all to, "Make sure you're really selling what the customer wants to buy." His philosophy was that his company was no longer in the business of just flying airplanes but was in the business of serving the travel needs of the public. And serving the travel needs of the public better than other companies was the secret to getting the business.

By stating "serving the travel needs of the public" as its organizing principle, Scandinavian Airlines allowed its employees to extend their job focus beyond their current customers to those who might become customers. It opened the narrow focus of their product from airline travel to the travel experience, which opened additional possibilities in terms of customers as well as products, and the company's approach to the market.

Is your organizing principle to sell product, or is it to enhance the lives of your customers? Does your customer-service effort minimize costs by avoiding customer complaints, or do your employees view these concerns as opportunities to improve service? When you think about it, do you even save money in the long run by avoiding customers? A major department-store chain has as its job description for its sales associates, "amaze the customer." Coupled with an empowering organizing principle, that is a job I am sure most people would enjoy having. This fits well with one of my basic principles of "happy employees are productive employees."

Don't allow your company to become introverted, looking inward and focusing on the problems of the process. This leads to avoiding your customers and an attitude of "if only these customers would just go away and leave me alone, I could get my job done." With more focus on the process than the customers, we run the risk of going down a different path than our customers are going. We all must remember it is for and because of the customer that we have a job.

Once we focus on our customers and really listen to what they are telling us, we can begin to see what they want in terms of customer experience. That customer experience is the basis of their buying motivation. We can then use our products, our product positioning, and our customer service to ensure that we deliver the customer experience they are seeking. We can expand our organizing principle to include not only our customers, but also those who are most likely to become our customers and begin providing the experience in a way it is not the outcome of our sales, but the source that leads to our sales.

I had a remarkable experience the other day. I was researching a new revenue vehicle online. For a particular site I had to register in order to see some of the more detailed information I was researching. As I got more information I found a feature where I could "chat" with a company rep about the product. I logged in and asked a question. Naturally my name came up on the chat screen with my message. My question was quickly answered by D. Best—Marketing Director. I typed in another question and sent it. Then my phone rang. The caller identified himself as Doug Best with whom I was chatting with online.

He had read my registration information, visited my company's Web site, and mentioned to me in the first several seconds of our conversation that his wife subscribed to one our magazines. All of this happened within a couple of minutes. Needless to say, I was impressed.

I spent a considerable amount of time talking to Mr. Best, and chances are I will be doing business with him in the not-too-distant future. His company's organizing principle of responsive customer service has impressed me as the type of company I want to work with. As a provider of such responsive services for my customers, this company not only has a good product to sell, but more importantly, they also practice what they preach.

Compare this to a competitor company whose site I actually visited earlier that day. The site did not ask for my name or information. It did not offer as much detail about their product, nor did it have a list of customers, FAQs, an example of the product, or any form of demonstration or interaction. It took me less than 15 seconds to view the three pages of their site and move on to another competitor, without sending an e-mail asking a salesperson to contact me. They truly were too busy to be bothered by a possible customer.

To survive and thrive in our current service economy, you must differentiate. Your unique qualities must stand out. To be "average" or "just as good as," really equates in the consumers' minds to being mediocre. And that is about the most devastating position on the product ladder a company can achieve. You are not even good enough at being bad to be at the very bottom. Nobody picks the second worst company to do business with, unless there are only two in the category.

Empower customer service. Jan Carlson's turnaround of Scandinavian Airlines was fueled by customer service. When empowered, his customer-service representatives were authorized to make it right for dissatisfied customers. He discovered that customers were not only reasonable in their requests for compensation for failed service, but that they really didn't expect to be compensated at all in many situations. These upset customers were as satisfied to talk to an employee who attempted to solve the problem, as they were to have the problem solved. They just wanted to be recognized and have their complaint heard with respect.

Walt Disney created the epitome of customer service with Disneyland. He told all his employees they were in show business. He maintained that company culture by calling his associates "cast members" and by drilling into each of their heads, "You are Disneyland." Every Disneyland employee knows that he or she may be a guest's only contact with a representative of the park. Each cast member is empowered to address guest concerns, and in turn, each person realizes how very important his or her performance is. A representative knows that he or she may only have a single chance to leave a lasting impression of a great Disneyland experience with each encounter. Imagine if your "cast members" had the same vision of customer interaction.

How much difference can this make? Consider this. Less than 4 percent of all customer complaints are ever voiced to the offending company. Over 96 percent just take their business to someone else. And as consumers we seldom identify with clarity what it takes to fully meet our expectations. But without a doubt we can tell the very instant when a company has crossed the line.

That customer needs and wants must be met are a given today. Anything less and you will be out of business. To compete, you really need to excel at meeting both. Today's business environment is far too unforgiving to be haphazard in customer service. To have "exceed customer expectations" as your verbal or written standard doesn't mean you can default to just meeting them. There is nothing extraordinary in just meeting expectations. And it's certainly no reason for a business to achieve only average (translate: mediocre) growth.

"Amaze the customer"—I like that from the customer-service side as well as the consumer point of view. It leaves no doubt what we expect the customer experience to be. As an operating principle it can be very empowering, and a good reason to jump rather than crawl out of bed every morning.

Why Magazines?

"The role of the publisher . . . has changed from seller of a product to consumers, to gatherer of consumers for advertisers . . . The role of the reader changes from sovereign consumer to advertiser bait."

— Vincent P. Norris

For many years, I was a radio/television broadcaster, living the heritage of Guglielmo Marconi and David Sarnoff. Many still acknowledge radio as the first unifying medium in mass communication. Television still stands as the single greatest advance in product promotion ever invented, by combining sight, sound and motion then delivering the message to the prospects home. Only after a career in broadcasting of more than twenty years did I defect to the print side of advertising.

In the mid-70s, radio broadcasting was still experiencing unprecedented growth and acceptance. For many advertisers the secret to success was just to advertise. Virtually any product had the ability to succeed with an adequate advertising budget. Television was combating radio's popularity among advertisers by developing the infomercial. Most magazines were broad-based and niche marketing was in its infancy.

As time passed, cable systems replaced the need for broadcast antennae across America. This period of growth was conducive to the creation of cable networks. Ted Turner's TBS was the first super-station, followed by a plethora of targeted niche networks. Broadcasting took its first step toward narrowing-casting leading toward the erosion of the big three TV network's dominance in the advertising industry.

Radio, sensing a weakness in television, surged under the guidance of the Radio Advertising Bureau to a much stronger position against other broadcast media. Magazines took note of the success of cable stations and started to aggressively develop profitable niche market publication models. The paradigm of smaller circulation magazines opened the door to advertisers who had previously relied upon less targeted media.

The dual strength of radio and magazines was short-lived as the Federal Communications Commission (FCC) deregulated the broadcast industry in the early 1980s. By rescinding its three-year ownership requirement, the FCC encouraged broadcast facilities to be bought and sold as commodities. As ownership changes and consolidation occurred, fewer radio and television stations focused on local programming. They began purchasing prepackaged programming in a broad-based generic version of entertainment, opening the door for magazines to continue to specialize in niche markets.

Today, magazines not only offer superior targeting ability for advertisers, but also offer more efficiency because, unlike broadcasters, publications have found how to serve smaller audiences economically.

I tell my staff they must answer four unasked questions for each of their advertisers. They are: "Why advertise?" "Why advertise in magazines?" "Why advertise in my magazine?" and "Why advertise in my magazine now?"

Too many advertising salespeople assume that potential advertisers are already aware of all the reasons to advertise in magazines. They do not realize how little time their clients spend thinking about advertising. After spending 50-60 hours each week considering the opportunities, problems and nuances of advertising, the typical salesperson expects his customer has done likewise and is therefore more advanced in his reasoning than he truly is. So the typical salesperson shortcuts to, "Do you want to buy?"

If you are reading this newsletter, you probably have several reasons to advertise. I hope your reasons for advertising are positive (advertising to achieve an end) and not negative (advertising to avoid a consequence). Any activity undertaken with the goal of avoiding a consequence is bound to feel obligatory and be an unsatisfactory experience. Alternatively, an activity undertaken to achieve a desired result can be much more invigorating and pleasurable.

Why advertising in magazines? Magazines engage the audience. With broadcast mediums of television and radio, the audience is passive in receiving the message with little more involvement than breathing. With magazines, the audience must read, interact and scan the pages to see the messages. Although a small factor, the tactile nature of magazines also engages the sense of touch. This adds another dimension to receiving the advertised message.

With niche publishing, magazines offer some of the best media targeting available today. Broadcast mediums cannot come close to targeting with the specificity of special interest publications. Entertainment, life style, project-based and reference-oriented content further increase the specificity of the audience.

Project-based publications offer strong advertising potential since subscribers buy these publications to complete one or two of the projects within the pages. They often keep these publications because they plan/hope to complete other projects in the future. Project-based magazines offer strong shelf life and some of the lowest pass-along readership numbers because of this very fact. This contributes to better advertising results as the same reader is exposed to an advertiser's message multiple times before the magazine is discarded or becomes out of date.

Pass-along readership that increases circulation does add reach for an advertiser's dollar. More often than not, the extended reach is at the expense of frequency. As a publication is passed along from reader to reader, the original subscriber and subsequent readers may only be exposed to an advertisement once, lowering the effectiveness of the advertising message.

We all know that the three best ways to increase advertising response rates is by lowering your product's price, increasing the number of exposures to your advertising message and by increasing the impact of your ad with visual stimulation. Finding ways to get more frequency without spending more or lowering margins gives the best profitability for your advertising dollar. So be cautious about magazines that have high pass-along readership. Project-based or reference-oriented magazines have the longest shelf life and give the best long-term value.

Niche market magazines also provide an endemic audience in many instances. A sewing or knitting magazine provides excellent targeting for a sewing or knitting product. Tight niche markets provide the most efficient exposure for highly specialized products. Broadcast and mass market mediums fail to deliver to these niche audiences and the pricing of their product includes a lot of waste. No medium can afford to only charge you for a portion of the audience delivered, so it is in your best interest to find the medium that matches your customer the best.

"Why advertise?" "Why advertise in magazines?" Hopefully you know a few more answers to these questions. "Why advertising in my magazine?" and "Why advertise in my magazine now?" Be sure your account manager takes the time to answer the last two questions to your satisfaction.

Marketing Research

Advertising is "the lubricant for the free-enterprise system."

— Leo-Arthur Kelmenson

"Marketing research" is a phrase almost every one of us has used at one time or another. It is a phrase that we throw around loosely and has different connotations to different people.

In preparing this chapter of the book I was reading the text book Marketing Research: An Applied Approach by Thomas C. Kinnear and James R. Taylor. Don't get me wrong: I do not do extensive research on what I write as most of it flows from my personal experiences in the advertising industry. In this case I was rereading some classic studies, looking for inspiration.

It struck me that many of us have a shared view of the concept of marketing research. However, very few of us really understand what it is and even a smaller number understand how to interpret research results. Research, no matter how thorough, is only as good as your ability to objectively interpret it within the context of your current situation.

In 1985, one of the world top marketing companies saw sales eroding to its major competitor and undertook a high profile market research project that asked consumers in a blind head-to-head test which product they preferred. After months of nationwide testing and discovering a marked preference for the competitor's product, the company decided to change the product to reflect the objective results of their research.

On April 23, 1985, in major test markets across the United States, including Indianapolis, the Coca-Cola Company launched "New

Coke." This was a sweeter version of the popular soft drink formulated to taste more like its competitor Pepsi Cola that was consistently beating Coke in blind taste tests. At the time, I was general sales manager of a soft rock radio station in Indianapolis, and was personally invited to the press conference and premiere of the new product. It was a spectacular event. To this day, I have never attended a more dramatic nor elaborate product introduction.

The next day, Coke loyalists by the thousands revolted and ran to the store to horde the old product. Old Coke clubs sprang up everywhere. It didn't matter that even these loyalists had not chosen Old Coke in the blind taste tests. There was a massive consumer revolt.

Seventy-eight days later, on July 11, 1985, Coca Cola announced they would resume production of the old Coke formula, to be known as Coca Cola Classic. They would continue to market the new formula under the Coke name to those they did convert. "We did not read the deep emotional ties that people had to the whole concept of Coca Cola," stated senior VP Brian Dyson in making the announcement.

More importantly, they failed to correctly interpret their own research in the context of their customer's experience and loyalty to the product. The New Coke story is a classic example of poor interpretation of marketing research. It took the Coca Cola Company many years and hundreds of millions of dollars to put that mistake behind them.

Understanding how and why people respond to questionnaires and surveys is a major key to getting useful information. People typically want to please the people who are interviewing them and skew their answers to where they believe the interviewer's interests lie.

In 1987, I commissioned Burns Media, Inc., of Los Angeles to do a focus group study of the radio market in South Bend, Indiana, where I was running a radio station. We arbitrarily selected listeners from my radio station and my nearest competitors to interview. Each respondent was told we were doing a "media study" and wanted their answers and opinions about local media. This was the typical one-way mirror study, with respondents answering questions on one side of the mirror and those of us commissioning the study on the other side, recording and listening to their unguarded answers.

Burns Media did a wonderful job of not letting respondents know who commissioned the study. In fact, they set up the interview area with strategically-placed note pads and coffee mugs from one of the local television stations. Each focus group was asked a series of open-ended questions about media. The majority of the questions were about television, leaving the respondents with the impression that the study was being conducted by a local television station. Only about thirty-five minutes of a two-and-a-half-hour meeting with each group was about radio. Those were thirty-five golden minutes because they gave us unguarded honest insights into what each wanted from their radio station. The results were interpreted and reported by professionals, and led to a major increase in market share for my station. It also taught me the vast difference between what people really want, and what they say they want, when asked by someone who can give it to them.

Armed with information like this, I hope you can see why I might be critical of advertisers who ask their customers questions in hopes of refining their advertising or marketing strategies. Human beings are too concerned with pleasing people in authority to be honest about what really motivates them. Their answers must be taken with a grain of salt - or at least an understanding of who they are, what they stand to gain with your approval and what they think you are attempting to find out.

In the 1987 study I mentioned above, we asked the focus group if traffic reports on radio in South Bend where needed. Almost all of them said no. South Bend was a small town with no perceived need for traffic information, and no radio station was providing any at that time.

The professionally-interpreted focus group report mentioned traffic reports as a key opportunity for radio stations. I programmed traffic reports several times a day during the morning and afternoon drive time beginning the next month. When the focus group study was repeated in 1988, with different respondents under the same conditions, my radio station's traffic reports were noted as one of the most important features offered by local radio.

Another important point about research and surveys is who you survey. More often than not you know what your customers like. After all, if you have a long term relationship with your customers, you must be doing something right. It is always good to survey their preferences from time to time. But do not confuse this type of research with what you need to do to increase your business. For that, you need to get answers from those who do not currently do business with you. That is the group that will offer you growth. Continually serving the core of your customer base without expanding who you are trying to reach will lead to a diminishing business.

There are many books written about market research. All of them are fairly logical in their approach and don't require rocket science to understand them. Unfortunately, too many non-marketing people attempt to run the marketing logic in their own heads and miss those little obvious things that make all the difference. All of them are fairly logical in their approach and don't require rocket science to understand them. Don't feel bad, though. You didn't decide to launch "New Coke."

Model for Growth

"Just because your ad looks good is no insurance that it will get looked at. How many people do you know who are impeccably groomed . . . but dull"?

— William Bernbach

When I talk to people about advertising, I always ask them about their plan to grow their business this year. I get answers like, "We'll grow a lot," or "We expect to grow as our product line expands." These answers tell me there is no strong plan behind their goal of business growth. If you ask me the same question, I will tell you the percentage and dollar amount by division. I will tell you when it will occur, where it will come from and how I know it came from that source. Why? Because I have a plan that I monitor every week and the ability to know if my plan is working or not.

In the last several chapters of ADvice, I have discussed several of the components needed to construct a model for growth for your business. Few businesses have a comprehensive plan for increasing sales. Those that do have a plan often fail to regularly monitor key metrics. This means they find out too late that their plan is not working.

First and foremost, you must take care of your established business. This means you must maintain advertising budgets, customer service, adequate inventory levels and all of the resources you utilized to build your current level of sales. Do not switch these resources to attract new business, as your base business will, slowly at first, begin to erode if you move these resources to court new customers.

National statistics tell us that over 15% of the population moves to a new residence every year. This means that in a matter of seven years, every one of your customers could move. For businesses doing only local business, knowledge of this factor is critical to staying in business. Additionally, people's habits change. Each year, people do more of the same things they did last year, and they also do less. Without doing an actual research study, let's assume some of your customers will consume more of your product, and others less. But those who do consume more will do so only if you continue to ask for their business and give them a good experience. And those who will consume less will consume much less than if you continually ask for their business.

It takes effort to maintain a customer base after you attain it. Don't make the mistake of taking your customers for granted. Every day, your competition is attempting to attract your customers. In this day and age, your competition is not limited to those in your industry. There are many companies vying for your customer's share of mind as well as a portion of their disposable income. Disney World considers everyone their competitor. In the book, Inside the Magic Kingdom, you will learn that Disney employees strive to make sure that their customer service is better than anyone, including Federal Express, and any other company that could gain a share of your customer's mind and budget.

As you have learned, you have some basic customer metrics. You have total number of transactions for the year and total sales revenues. By dividing your revenue by the number of transactions, you determine your average transaction. If your sales were $1,000,000 and you had 10,000 transactions, your average transaction was $100. Multiply your average transaction by the number of times each customer buys yearly, and you have 'value per customer.' In the case above, if your average customer makes 5 purchases per year, the average customer value is $500. And, your customer base is about 2,000 customers.

Now comes the fun part. How much do you want your company to grow? How much more business do you want in the next year than you had in the last year? Let's say for this example you want to grow your business by 20%. That means an additional $200,000 in sales. How do you go about doing it? First, you will need 2,000 additional average transactions of $100. But you will only need an additional 400 customers to achieve this.

Where do you find 400 additional customers? If you remember the first chapter of ADvice titled "Big Fish, Little Fish" we talked about dominating your current advertising mediums before moving on to new options. The average magazine, newspaper, radio station, or television station has more readers, listeners or viewers than you will ever need. You have established a foothold in your current medium and it will be much easier to leverage your growth budget in your current medium to attract your new customers from familiar territory.

It is a mistake to try to grow using the shotgun effect of buying a little bit in every conceivable media option, or attempting to purchase the largest circulation or audience. This is very expensive, and you must compete with those companies that already have established their brand with that audience. Not only is this inefficient, it seldom achieves the desired results. Reaching 1,000,000 people once is not as effective as reaching 50,000 people 10 times. And the latter takes half as much money. It is very cost efficient to remember that you do not need to reach everyone with your message in order to grow your business. You just need to reach a targeted audience with enough repetition to motivate them to sample your product.

How big of an audience do you need? Out of 100 consumers in your market, how many buy your product? If that number is 1 out of 20, then your market share is approximately 5%. You need to target a universe of 20 times the number of new customers you need. In the above example where 400 customers will account for your sales growth, you need an audience of 8,000. Don't make the mistake of approaching an audience much larger than you need for your 400 new customers. You probably won't have the budget required to purchase the repetition needed to generate action.

Even so, you must realize that new customer acquisition is twice as expensive as customer maintenance. Be prepared to spend money to lure new business your way. Make your best product offers to generate these new sales. Do whatever you need to do in order to make the new sales, and give world class service to these customers in order to get them to return. Remember the annual value of a customer. Spending $100 to generate $100 in sales is well worth it, if you convert that person to a $500 annual value.

Establish your maintenance and growth plans, watch your metrics and count your new customers as they come in. If you have a plan to maintain your established business, a separate plan to attract new customers, and a strategy for each, they will be relatively easy to monitor.

Before you can generate growth intentionally, you need to know how much you intend to grow your business, how long that growth will take, where the growth will come from, and how much you will need to invest to achieve the growth. A strong advertising strategy, coupled with good products and customer service, gives you the very best opportunity to grow your business and your bottom line.

Lessons learned

"Always vote for principle, though you may vote alone, and you may cherish the sweetest reflection that your vote is never lost."

— John Quincy Adams

I started ADvice several years ago to share some of the lessons I have learned about advertising over the years. My hope is that by reading about my experiences, others might avoid some of the many inevitable pitfalls in advertising.

A good friend once joked that, today, "instant gratification is not fast enough." He said this in jest but there is a lot of truth to his words. Years ago, in an entrepreneurial role, I talked to potential investors about funding for a business. Many of these investors expected extraordinary returns. Most want a majority share in the business, triple digit returns and an unreasonable timetable. Why? Because an earlier investor decided he wanted better returns than the last guy. So he pressed the entrepreneur to get more profit out of the business plan. The investor got what he wanted. The next investor asked for more and got it too.

As the required returns for new ventures escalated, so did the basic premise of the business. Finally a point was reached where the business could not provide the return. In fact the required return is the factor that made the business fail. It failed, not because it was not a good idea, but because the investor required more than it could deliver. But in the eyes of the always-arrogant investor, the business was determined to be a high risk.

Because some businesses have now shown they can fail, investors have asked for higher returns to offset the added risk. This puts pressure on entrepreneurs to provide even more optimistic predictions that lead to a higher failure rate and, yes, increased demands because of increased risk. This is the mentality that leads to things like Enron. If everyone could only get rich over a reasonable period of time, instant gratification would be a wonderful and unique thing.

Our fanatical obsession with beating the next guy, however, has led to compromised ethics, compromised rules, and even breaking the law. When I look at how much money a person or business can make by the simple compounding of consistent yearly profits, I cannot understand why so many want 100%, 150% and 200% increases at the expense of sound business practices.

Think about the guys from Enron. Top management there was making more money in a year than many of us will ever make in our lifetimes, but that wasn't enough. Stockholders wanted more, executives wanted more. Unrealistic greed led to compromising the rules, then to breaking the rules and finally to breaking the law. In the end, not only did the greedy lose, but thousands of others did too.

There was a famous television commercial years ago for the brokerage firm of Smith Barney that featured the actor John Houseman. The tag line was memorable. Houseman, with his proper diction, looked directly into the camera and said, "They make their money the old fashioned way. They earn it."

The investor/entrepreneur relationship is often duplicated by the advertiser and advertising salesperson. The advertiser demands more and the salesperson promises to deliver more. Eventually the demands exceed what is possible to deliver. The victim here ends up being credibility of advertising as a whole. Some ad salespeople are so intimidated they willingly promise more than they know they can deliver. Other salespeople will not admit that their product cannot measure up to the exaggerated promises of their competitors. Finally, some advertisers force salespeople to make unrealistic assurances in order to make a purchase. All three scenarios undermine the relationship between buyer and seller.

If you are an advertiser, do not believe that, just because the product is yours, its sales performance will outpace Coca-Cola because of advertising. I never cease to be amazed by the number of new businesses I encounter who honestly believe they will have record sales resulting from spending nothing more than pocket change on advertising.

Reasonable people starting a business will readily admit their lack of experience in every area but advertising. Many of these entrepreneurs believe that since they watch television commercials, read magazine ads and listen to Coke commercials on the radio, they know how to advertise. In spite of their admitted ignorance in every other area, even more believe they can achieve advertising success by doing less than anyone else. As with every other aspect of your business, get advice from a professional and invest enough to achieve your goal.

Advertising salespeople are motivated by the same things as everyone else: wanting to be liked, to be seen as helpful and wanting to be appreciated. They also want to be the ones you buy advertising from. In today's highly competitive marketplace, those desires can frequently lead to exaggeration and, occasionally, misinformation. As a manager I do not condone it nor encourage it. As a salesperson I face the same temptations every day.

Find a salesperson you can trust. Work with them. Test their reliability from time to time to make sure they are working for you rather than working you. A good salesperson will have your goals in mind. A great salesperson will spend more time talking to you about selling your product than selling you his product.

Don't feel the need to become an advertising expert. You need to focus on running your business. Find an advertising salesperson you trust, one who is concerned with helping your business grow. If the salesperson is concerned only with selling advertising to you, his business will thrive more than yours will.

Finally, think about how much is enough. Several magazines published by my company have circulation of over 100,000. There are other magazines with whom we compete that have circulation far more than that. Very few businesses could handle that volume of businesses. If 100,000 customers we standing at the door of your store tomorrow morning when you opened for business and it took 5 seconds for you to greet each person as they walked through the door, it would take nearly 139 hours or over two weeks of general business hours for them to walk into your business. Since the average cash register transaction takes about 90 seconds, it would over 2,499 hours to ring up a sale for each of these customers.

Yet many advertisers would rather spend more money to reach more people, when they are already reaching enough. If the advertising message sent is just a little better then it does not take as many people to give the desired result.

A strong selling message is the most effective lever you have. I can cite hundreds of examples of where offers go unanswered even though they were put in front of millions of people versus hundreds of responses to an offer shared with only a thousand or so prospects. Because the advertiser's concern for reaching a large number of people, was not balanced with giving those people a reason to try his product over all others. Think about it: as an advertiser you pay for every person reached. Why not make sure every person reached reacts to your ad before you try to reach more people? Improving your advertising message is a small cost compared to the cost of doubling the number of people seeing it. Advertisers need to remember, "You don't need them all, you only need enough."

What works better than a low price?

"We want consumers to say, 'That's a hell of a product' instead of, 'That's a hell of an ad.'"

— Leo Burnett

This morning I spent an hour and a half on a weekly conference call. The purpose of this regular call is training for some of my newer salespeople. What we discussed turned out to be very interesting to us, and will hopefully be very helpful to you, a potential advertiser of ours.

We talked about all of the facets of an advertisement that impacts the results from running the ad. You see, I spend an inordinate amount of my time talking about the things advertisers talk about with my salespeople, that is, advertising rates. How are they justified, arrived at, and calculated? They are higher than, the same as, or totally unreasonable as compared to someone's hearsay version of what is available out there.

First let me say, the old saying, "If you have to ask how much it is, you probably can't afford it," holds some truth. Anyone that believes a publisher can print a page of advertising or editorial, and distribute it through subscriptions and/or newsstand sales to thousands of people for a buck, is sadly mistaken. Every page we print and mail has a definite and constantly rising cost structure. (By the way, the politicians we have voted into our government have decided that advertising that is being sent through the United States Postal Service should cost more than virtually all other postal-delivered matter. So calling your congressman might be your best course of action the next time you face an advertising rate increase.)

But the saddest state of affairs is that advertisers are aggressive about and focus an inordinate amount of time in discussing this one facet -- advertising space rates -- that has the least amount of impact on advertising response. The list of items we discussed in our meeting, complete with examples of the good, the bad and the ugly are what my salespeople are studying right now.

Each month I hear from a selection of advertisers who say that our magazines don't work. The statement is inaccurate and taken at face value places blame on the media and not the message. First let me say that regardless of what any advertiser believes, my magazines do work. They are printed on paper as we have promised. They contain a palatable mixture of editorial content and advertising messages as promised. The majority of our magazines are delivered via U.S. mail to our list of subscribers, while some others are sold via a newsstand distribution system to non-subscribing readers as promised.

Stating that one of our magazines does not work is like sending a letter to Bill Gates asking for $1 million, and when you do not get the money, then saying the post office doesn't work. Believe me, like the post office, we pretty much know that your ad was delivered with our publication. To put it kindly, maybe your advertising message placed in our magazine was not as compelling as needed for the results expected.

Compelling? What makes an ad compelling? Maybe it is the price-value equation. Does the perceived value of your offer entice my reader to take action? Is your message customer-focused? Are you providing a solution to a significant problem or fulfilling an acknowledged need? Are you using testimonials from satisfied customers to tout the benefits of your product? How about a call to action? Are you asking for the order and giving sufficient reason to "call today!"

It is appalling that nearly half of the ads we receive for our publications have weak copy points, hard-to-find contact information, use grossly exaggerated product claims that undermine credibility, and contain a variety of other equally obvious shortcomings.

Too many inexperienced advertisers feel the answer to making an ad successful and cost-effective is to expect it to do the job of several ads and sell multiple products. Too much information is even more confusing than not enough. White space in an ad gives the eye freedom to focus, and the mind room to comprehend.

In today's world, clutter is the last thing your ad should portray. A busy ad will be skipped over more quickly than a blank page. My salespeople and I discussed a list of several one-word and one-image ads that are classics in their ability to portray a singular message with one word and a picture.

Advertisers should separate themselves from their products enough to fully explain the benefits that are imparted and that they take for granted. But they need to remember, consumers want solutions not features. I don't care about ball bearings. I care about whether the stand swivels smoothly, requiring little effort. I don't care about the forging process of the high-tensile steel frame. A lifetime replacement guarantee is more than adequate for my needs.

Size matters. Regardless of what we want to think, bigger ads sell more. The Magazine Publishers of America organization regularly commissions studies to index reader recall of different ad sizes and placement within magazines. Oddly enough, the indexing of these response rates corresponds almost identically with advertising rate structures. The bottom line is: You pay more -- you get more.

Copy testing takes such little time and really does not require a lot more than common sense to interpret. At our company a direct-response marketer tests every sales piece we send to consumers, we are constantly testing copy, multiple-purchase offers, payment terms, fulfillment terms, discounts versus premiums, and many other marketing variables. At any one time we may be testing three to six variables. We then focus our efforts and major investment on the message that tests as the strongest.

In all of my years at this company, fewer than five advertisers have suggested they need to test copy. During the same period thousands have suggested that my advertising rates are too high. I don't mind, it is part of how our industry works. Poor advertising salespeople discount rates because they do not know how to make poor ads into more effective ads. Even when an ad salesperson knows how to improve an ad, there are far too many advertisers unwilling to listen.

Salespeople follow where advertisers take them. And today there is an almost universal race to get to the lowest possible rate structure possible. Still many ads don't work as well as expected. With this continued inattention to the factors that impact advertisement effectiveness, "free" is going to become too expensive in the near future.

I've asked my salespeople to spend as much time talking about product features and benefits in ad copy as they do about show specials, frequency discounts and limited-time offers, because if the copy does not generate a sale, no price is good. However, if the time spent on copy points improves response rates by 10 or 20 percent, it may be the most valuable time spent by the client and the salesperson.

What works better than a low price? Part 2

"One-third of the people in the United States promote, while the other two-thirds provide."

— Will Rogers

I received about as much feedback from our last newsletter titled "What works better than a low price?" as any in recent memory. Apparently many of you saw the wisdom of making your ads more effective as an important part of your advertising plan. So I thought it might serve us all well if I continued that discussion in this chapter of ADvice.

Let's get to point: What is your advertising strategy? Do you have one? In each magazine chapter, I encounter dozens of ads where it is obvious that there is no specific strategy for the ad. I also encounter others where a strategy is used, but only because the ad concept was copied from someone else who thoughtfully employed the original strategy. Too often, the imitator's product does not fit the strategy, even though the ad looks good. Using someone else's advertising strategy can be as distasteful as using someone else's toothbrush. (Note how effective, strong analogies make a point.)

"Positioning" is a concept and term made popular in the 1970s by Al Ries and Jack Trout. It is a strategy of comparing your product to something that is well-known and claiming a "position" relative to something that is familiar to your target audience. One of the better-known positioning campaigns was 7UP's "uncola" campaign. Without mentioning the two soft-drink giants of Coca Cola and Pepsi, 7UP was able to slingshot its sales and market share into third place by creating a position that was associated with, but definitely not the same as the top two market segments in the soft-drink industry.

Likewise, Avis Car Rental put major distance between itself and other competitors while closing the gap on Hertz with its slogan, "We're number two, and we try harder." Before this campaign Avis, like many other rental agencies, was of little consequence to Hertz, the industry giant. Positioning brought Avis so close to the No. 1 company, that it eventually dropped the "We're number two," and now it uses only the "we try harder" portion of the positioning statement.

The strength of the positioning concept is the knowledge that even with some effort the average human mind can remember a list of only about seven items in a category. Usually the top two or three are easiest to remember and have been "positioned" by natural selection or default. Unfortunately the remaining four or five are usually indistinguishable and suffer by having a weak image. Through positioning you can place your brand in a new and separate category where you establish the dominant position. Not only is your company or product easier to remember, it is also the top competitor in the new category.

Positioning also allows a relatively unknown product to immediately gain credibility by comparing itself to a commonly known product in another category. The book Positioning: The Battle for Your Mind by Trout and Ries is a classic in the study of advertising strategy.

In the 1970s, Madison Avenue, the self-professed seat of advertising creativity, began segmenting markets according to a study called VALS, which stood for Value And Lifestyle Study. VALS broke consumers into five different groups based upon their consumer habits, socio-economic backgrounds and emotional makeups. These psychographic distinctions led to a different approach to the selling of soap. Belongers, Emulators, Emulator-Achievers, Societally Conscious Achievers and the Need-Directed were the five consumer groups whose different makeups demanded different approaches in order to sell them products.

Belongers, the largest group, include one out of three people. It is not hard to imagine the type of appeal needed to attract these potential consumers. The psychographic traits of this group are traditional and conservative. Mainline products like Coca Cola, Pepsi, Budweiser and McDonalds are staples of this group.

Emulators are about 15 percent of the population and will do just about anything to fit in. Most of them carry childhood insecurities that lead them to buy products which invite acceptance. They buy the coolest product to compensate for their low self-image with hopes that the product will make up for their personal shortcomings, whether real or imagined. This group was the target of many cigarette ads featuring celebrities and strong images like the Marlboro Man.

Emulator-Achievers have already arrived. They are the 20 percent of the population that drive Mercedes, drink expensive champagne, shop at Gucci and Tiffany's as well as regularly upgrade their belongings to the latest technology. Although affluent, most Emulator-Achievers have not received the level of affluence they feel they deserve, which makes them perfect targets for products that speak success. This is the group that put Ralph Lauren and Izod, with their logos of polo players and alligators, on the map.

Societally Conscious Achievers were the flower children of the baby-boom generation who are more concerned about their own inner peace and the environment than their financial or material success. Also 20 percent of the population, they would rather buy from socially responsible companies and buy socially responsible products. This is the market that popularized L.L. Bean, Honda and Volvo. The drink lighter wines, herbal tea and created the market for bottled waters. A much more elusive target than other psychographic categories, these consumers are not swayed by overt advertising messages. They are more into supporting movements and will buy products that are congruent and compatible with political positions. Also a part of the 1970s fitness movement, this group is big into exercise.

Need-Directed are the 15 percent of the population and are best-defined as survivors. From an advertising perspective they are a non-market. They find themselves so driven to make ends meet that brand differentiation is of little consequence to them. The Need-Directed are not driving new cars, buying branded clothing, acquiring state-of-the-art technology or even taking the family out for a fast meal.

Understanding the emotions, needs and drivers of the different psychographic categories leads to offering different appeals to sell products to them. Matching your products to these needs is a basic way to reach and serve specific consumer groups.

Understanding what you are selling also is a key to enhancing advertising results. Charles Revson, founder of Revlon Cosmetics, once said, "In our factory, we make lipstick. In our advertising, we sell hope." Consumers generally do not buy products. They buy solutions to their problems, security for a financial future, or satisfaction for unfulfilled urges. Too many advertisers assume that consumers understand their own problems. Usually they do not. Many times consumers do not even know there is a problem. Often they sense that something is missing. They cannot and more importantly, will not, purchase your solution until they see or perceive a need and believe your product provides the result they desire in their future.

My staff sells advertising. I know without a shadow of doubt that not one of my customers wants to buy advertising. As a matter of fact, I can say with almost total certainty that given the choice, every one of my customers would never buy advertising again. However, each and every one of them wants the results that in most cases only advertising can deliver. Their desire for these positive results outweighs their lack of desire to buy advertising. We make it easier to buy our product, I hope, by being conscious of what our customers are trying to achieve, and by providing professional guidance and direction, to help them achieve those goals.

Let me give you a list of what Charlie Brower, former president and CEO of Batten, Barton, Durstine and Osborn Inc., says turns people on and off to advertising:

What turns people off to advertising:

1. Talking like a pitchman instead of like a friend.
2. Not knowing when to shut up.
3. Using too many sales points so they remember none.
4. Talking about the product instead of what it will do for the reader.
5. Being too important about a product of small importance.
6. Being too urgent ... too "hurry! hurry! hurry!"
7. Making unbelievable and unsupported claims.
8. Being confusing.
9. Making the reader work to get your message.
10. Being just plain silly.
11. Worst of all -- being dull.

People are turned on to your advertising by:

1. Friendly help -- but not too friendly. Nobody wants you to wag your tail.
2. Simplicity (consider that as the impact of the word written ten times over).
3. Wit, but not clowning.
4. Real news, but not fake news.
5. Advertisements that reward reading.
6. A logical development of a single idea.
7. Service suggestions (how to use).
8. New uses for familiar products.
9. Interest, even borrowed interest.

Back to Fundamentals

"Most people have the will to win; few have the will to prepare to win."

— Bobby Knight

I attended Indiana University in Bloomington as a freshman in 1969 and became a diehard Hoosier hoops fan. Yes, I am one of those basketball fanatics who still bemoans the loss of Bob Knight as Indiana University's basketball coach. My son, who is now into his 40's, attended the Bob Knight basketball camp when he was in grade school.

One big reason I am a Bob Knight fan is that he builds his players' skills and his team's strategy upon sound fundamentals. You must be proficient in the basics before you can graduate to more advanced levels. And, when your game plan goes awry, going back to the basics is a very good way to solve your problems quickly.

My view of business is very similar to Bob Knight's view of basketball. I believe that there are some universal basics that must be mastered before you can, or should, move on to more advance levels. At the foundation of a business is the fact that you must spend, sell and keep. You must spend money to develop a product or service, you must then sell your product or service to a market and from the first two, you must create a reserve to keep.

Like any championship team, a business needs a clear-cut vision and definition of winning. Everyone on the team needs to have the same common goal. But these goals need to be grounded in the fundamentals of business. The first building block of a business is to make a profit or to end up with more money than you started with. This is created by spending less than you make.

After you've spent money to create your product, you need to sell that product at a price that covers your costs, with some left over. What can you do if you are not making a profit? There are two solutions: cutting your expenses or increasing your sales revenue. Profit is the difference between what you spend and the revenue from your sales. Cutting costs while maintaining revenue will increase your profit, as will increasing sales revenue while maintaining costs.

There are lots of folks who think they can create profits by cutting costs. Watching expenses is certainly a wise way of running your business. But very few companies have cut their way to success. Cutting expenses is not a long-term growth strategy. When your business future is based upon cutting your expenses, you are missing the big opportunity of capitalism: limitless income from a free market economy.

The other way to increase profits is by generating more sales revenue. You can increase sales revenues by selling customers more or selling more customers. Selling each customer more product increases the value of each transaction. Selling the same amount to more different customers increases the number of transactions. Both of these strategies are best achieved through the application of sound advertising principles, as we discussed in previous issues. Of course, this all presupposes that you have structured your sales model to be profitable.

You must have a solid business model or you may be doomed from the start. There is a classic story of two young men from Ohio who were out to make money so they drove their pick-up truck down to Georgia in the early summer and bought enough watermelons at $24 a dozen to fill up the bed of their pick-up truck. They then drove back north to sell the watermelon and make their fortune. In short order they sold every one of them for $1.00 a piece. When they counted their money, they discovered that they only had half of their original investment. Upon pondering the situation, they agreed in order to make their business grow, they needed a larger truck. And so it goes more often than we want to believe in many businesses. The solution we pick has little to do with the problem we face.

A mentor of mine once told me that profits cover a multitude of sins. He should have said that no matter how much talent you have, a lack of profits will always expose even your most harmless fault. Few of us could survive the constant scrutiny of our faults, no matter how small.

I used to work for a publishing company that had as many as 50 revenue-generating programs. We had an elaborate financial model with metrics and ratios all designed to tell us how well our business was doing. Each month we spent endless hours, it seems, preparing reports to tell us one thing: did we end up with more money at the end of the month than we had in the beginning? Our financial reviews were very detailed and required lots of time in order to answer a few questions. Did we meet our forecast? If not, what were doing in order to meet it in the future? If we did meet our forecast, what were doing to sustain it?

I joked that if our company were a basketball team, we would have five players on the floor, 30 statisticians charting each play, and a team of writers preparing the play-by-play report for the senior strategy consortium. That consortium creates a plan for our management team to implement, through the technical coaching department, within budget restrictions, utilizing our precisely formatted forms and QS9000-audited processes of improvement. This, of course, is a tongue in cheek exaggeration, but it does point out that it is easily possible for the focus of business to not be where it needs to be, on creating a profit.

Returning to fundamentals, making money starts on the front end. You must build a profitable business model. Like our Ohio partners above, if there is a flaw in your basic business model, an increase in sales will only magnify the problem. Is your business model profitable? Do you have a few basic metrics to reliably measure it? Do you have the tools to adjust your business model if you are not achieving your forecast? Can you build a foundation for your model that sustains success when you are achieving your business forecast?

Dribbling and shooting, guarding and rebounding and understanding the flow of the game, are the some of the basics of basketball. With these few areas mastered you can have a lot of fun. Without understanding them, you will find it hard to even play the game. The same is true with business. You must know the rules. You must know how to make the plays and make adjustments to the way you play the game. After all, management of a business is no more than applying minor adjustments to the current situation until the desired degree of profitability is attained. Champions in business continue to practice the fundamentals over and over, always getting them right.

Business is a like a competitive game. At its best, it gets your competitive juices flowing. At its worst, it can beat you up badly. And in business, it is good to remember that whether you own the team or you are just a player, winning is as important in your business as it may be in any game of basketball.

How not to plan

"The Death of Advertising? I think that's in the book of Revelation. It's the day when people everywhere become satisfied with their weight, their hair, their skin, their wardrobe, and their aroma."

— Jef I. Richards

As a sales manager I shudder each time I hear that one of my salespeople has a plan. The conversation often goes like this, "I have a quota of $20,000, so all I need to do sell is four $5,000 packages." Believe it or not, knowing exactly what to do is one of the best ways to miss your goal. I can recount hundreds of sales stories about salespeople who designed perfect plans to make their goals and failed.

It is a funny thing about human nature -- we hold onto those things that made us look good in the past. Usually the reason we look good is because we did something new and different. So what do we do? We repeat it, not because it is new and different, but because the results it generated brought us recognition. The acclaim from those successes has a way of locking us into processes. Sometimes these processes become outdated, but our former success and our familiarity with the operation keep us right where we are. As soon as a successful process becomes a habit, it is more like an anchor, preventing our progress, than a support.

In times of making a plan we all ask ourselves questions. If I do this, then what happens? Then what is next? Our mind-set in virtually every case is linear. Each action moves us forward, as if the shortest distance between two points is a straight line. Wouldn't life be great if everything we did was this simple? Unfortunately life is not a linear path. It is very circuitous. You start out in one direction, and before you reach your destination, you will likely see the horizon from all points on the compass. That's just how it goes. Why then are we surprised when our linear plan doesn't work? This is the ultimate in practicing something over and over, expecting it to be different each time. Most of us adjust by not really believing in our plan. Some even decide planning is not in their best interest to do since frustration is the fruit of more than just a few elaborate plans. We only think of achieving our goal by getting from here to the result as a straight line.

Years ago, I took a very expensive and intensive management course with multi-day sessions occurring in San Francisco, Dallas, New York, Chicago and finally ending in Philadelphia. We were taught that the art of management was getting from where we were to where we wanted to be -- no matter what. We also learned that no matter how comprehensive the plan, there comes a time when it stops working. For most, that is when the commitment to the goal waivers and a negotiation with the promised results happens.

This is also the point when most people learn to hate plans because, short of lowering the promised results, we think the only alternative to our dilemma is to work our original plan harder. After going through this once, no wonder people hate to make plans. What once seemed only a path to predictable results becomes an albatross around our necks that we cannot seem to shed. I know many people experience this because every time I ask my staff for their plan, I see it in their eyes, hear it in their voices, and even sense it in their body language that they are feeling trapped. Remember, most people think of plans in a linear fashion. Even though we fail to include them in the process, we all know at least one and probably several roadblocks will appear in the path to our goal.

Quitting or working harder is not the answer. Where is the problem? The plan is not working. So stop and go on to plan B, or if there is no plan B, as in many cases, create one. And please don't make plan B just more of plan A. This is the shortest distance to frustration you will find. It is certain to sustain your unfulfilled expectations. Better yet, just announce that your plan does not work. The declaration itself gives you a sense of freedom. This freedom will give you the ability to brainstorm and apply out-of-the-box thinking, which will help you achieve a creative solution. Remember your second plan is likely to be linear too. So save unused ideas that might be helpful with plan C should the need arise.

Life is not straight lines or direct courses to the goals or destinations we seek. Every one of them is filled with curves and detours that can be exciting and exhilarating if you do not allow getting pushed off course to stifle your expectations. Understanding that something will come up to derail your commitment prepares you to handle these diversions in a calm, rational manner. When these things disrupt us, and we react adversely, as if we did not expect them, life is in control, and we are just reacting to it. But when we are aware that these bumps will appear out of nowhere, we can be proactive in addressing them when they do, and we remain in control of our life and our plans.

So when it comes to making plans, I routinely use the phrase "over-structure." I advise everyone to make your plan bigger than the goal requires. Then when the unexpected occurs, you already have in place the momentum, the structure and/or the flexibility to address the inevitable interference and still reach your goal. Nobody ever succeeded consistently with a plan just big enough to reach their goal.

Learning how to make effort, the plan and resource consumption the variables in reaching our goals is learning how to become effective no matter what. It really becomes simple once you understand that all of the pieces of the plan can be changed -- not just the results. Input, mixture, catalysts and various other aspects can be adjusted to the current state of activity to generate a constant output or result. The same can be said for advertising and marketing of products. There are many variables that you can manipulate in the equation to acquire the desired output. But you must be prepared to say that the plan in not working in order to gain the freedom to creatively adjust the formula and achieve your goal output.

When I was a young man, my father constantly challenged me to find several different ways to achieve the same goal. He made a game out of it by asking me how many different ways I could accomplish a task. Since that time, I think in terms of multiple mechanics. Then I find the most reasonable as the probable first plan. After completing the management course I mentioned earlier, I now save the alternatives for plans B, C and D, should I need them, if the first plan does not generate the outcome I intended.

The true secret, I believe, in achieving success rests in not being married to the plan, but in being unwavering in your commitment to the outcome. In the long run, I think this offers far more freedom than being locked into a specific set of actions. We just have to be cognizant that it is human nature to hold on to those things in which we have invested our time and treasure. Holding on too long to a plan that isn't working can be a large contributing factor to missing your goal. It takes practice to know how and when to change. But that is also a great deal of the fun.

Holiday Advertising

"The very first law in advertising is to avoid the concrete promise and cultivate the delightfully vague."

— Bill Cosby

As we find ourselves at the end of the year, I felt it most appropriate to talk about holiday advertising in the chapter of ADvice. My reason is that few will take heed unless they are feeling the pangs of unfulfilled sales expectations right now.

A goodly portion of retailers generate as much as 40% of their annual revenues between Thanksgiving and the end of the year. This fact should give new meaning to 'holiday cheer.' For many, it will determine if you had a great year, or just a so-so year.

One of my first holiday advertising experiences with retailers was a photo finishing company. In 1977, same-day photo labs were just beginning to appear across the country. One of these was an advertising client of mine in Bloomington, Indiana where I was the sales manager for a local radio station.

My client and I met in September to talk about their holiday advertising schedule. I was confident that I was going to sell them a large schedule during the very crowded period from Thanksgiving to Christmas. Boy was I wrong. My account lowered his regular high frequency schedule to a minimal maintenance schedule for the period beginning the first day of November through Christmas Day.

Unlike other advertisers, though, he bought two commercials per hour beginning the day after Christmas and running through the middle of January. When I asked him why he was advertising that way, he told me that nearly half of the consumer photo-finishing business occurred each year during the six-week period beginning the first of January. This schedule was very successful, and not only because of its timing. He advertised all year long. He did not spend big dollars to compete in a highly competitive period that was not his strongest selling season, but he did advertise.

Holiday advertising works best when you have laid the groundwork by advertising your business all year. During the holiday season, consumers tend to spend more money with trusted and familiar advertisers than they do with someone who just waits to advertise once per year.

This year, major retailers who anticipated lagging sales drove results by aggressively discounting earlier in the season, a practice that is happening more and more each year. Until last year, "Black Friday," the day after Thanksgiving, was the largest shopping day of the year. Because of the expanding practice of offering deep discounts during the last few shopping days, Christmas Eve became last year's biggest day. Consumers are getting wiser each year and forcing retailers to give even better discounts during the last few days.

It makes you wonder who is driving sales. Today, the consumer is driving sales. Years ago when retailers started promoting Christmas and offering discounted prices to get those last few dollars before year's end, consumers learned the rules of the game. Now they wait until the price drops to a level that equates to a real value in their eyes. Unfortunately, major retailers have to continue and play the game or run the risk losing sales to their competitors.

How do you get your fair share of holiday sales, yet avoid the radical discounting game played by major retailers? One answer is to advertise all year long. During the holiday rush, consumers more often spend their money with trusted and familiar retailers. You can help the consumer avoid the rush by promoting gifts outside the Thanksgiving-Christmas period. Encourage layaway or pre-order programs. Sometimes you can offer personalized or limited availability items that require a longer production cycle. These purchases may need to be made prior to the yearly heavy discounting period.

Understand that getting the consumer to consider your product as a gift purchase in addition to their personal use increases the sales potential for everyone that buys from you. Offer additional services for early purchases. Some times these value-added incentives will generate sales prior to the holiday rush.

Run gift sales in August or September where the consumer can purchase several gift items and get a discount on their personal purchase. They will find it easier to buy something for themselves when they are receiving discounts for buying Christmas gifts at the same time.

Always tie emotion to your advertising message and sell the experience your product gives the consumer. Avoid price comparisons for as long as possible, although price will have to be addressed. As you become better at selling the experience, price will not be the controlling factor that it is with major retailers during the holidays.

Teach your consumers to buy value, not price. Build value all year long by advertising the features and benefits of your product. When you do not build the value equation, you only have price as a way to generate purchasing action.

Differentiate your product from the rest of the pack by adding value. Add value by using "cause marketing." Donate a portion of proceeds to a charity or cause for a specified period. It does not need to be a significant percentage, nor for a long period, to demonstrate that your company cares. A local grocery chain in my area gives 1% of a weekend's proceeds to the American Cancer Society and gets incredible sales and press from the effort.

The bottom line is that holiday sales results come from being a company everyone wants to do business with all year long. To make your year based on holiday sales is short-sighted and too little, too late. If you come into the fourth quarter and need a miracle to make your year, you've already lost, big time. And if by chance, you make it work, you will soon find yourself in the same position as the major retailers. In a very short time, you will only be able to needed generate sales without offering major discounts. Consumers will have learned that they don't have to buy your product at full price, because you have demonstrated that your willingness to cut prices to finally sell something. The best way to win this game is to avoid the temptation and not play.

Top 10

"If we listened to our intellect, we'd never have a love affair. We'd never have a friendship. We'd never go into business, because we'd be cynical. Well, that's nonsense. You've got to go jump off cliffs all the time and build your wings on the way down."

— Ray Bradbury, author

Over the three-plus decades I have been in advertising, I have heard numerous explanations from business people as to why they don't advertise. These "reasons" are almost always given in total sincerity, and sadly enough, with the earnest belief that they matter. I am sharing them with you as a matter of humor, for if you don't view these with humor, the very sad future that they portend makes you sad for the people who said them.

The number **10** reason for not advertising: **"Everybody knows me."** The first time I encountered this reason for not spending money on advertising, it came from a business person who was 15 years my senior. I accepted the reason for the time being and left. After thinking about it a couple of days, I went back to see the business person. I asked him if he still felt that way, and he said yes. So I challenged him to pick up the telephone book and give me 10 random numbers. I bet him that at least half would not know who he was. He took the bet. I was wrong. None of the ten knew of the business. We called twenty numbers before we found one that had heard of this local business. I was right, he was wrong, but he still didn't advertise.

The number **9** reason for not advertising: **"I don't have any money."** Now this is a very good "reason" to share with a salesperson that is paid on commission. If the customer doesn't pay his bill, the salesperson will have done a lot of work only to not get paid in the end. But the bigger question is this, "If you don't do something to generate business, and hence turn your inventory into cash, how are you ever going to pay all of your other bills?" Not having any money is the perfect reason to advertise.

The number **8** reason for not advertising: **"Advertising does not work."** Two words Mr. Prospect -- Coca Cola. Anyone who can say that advertising does not work, and then with a straight face buy any commercial product risks being the biggest hypocrite in the world. This often goes to the core of a person's feelings of inadequacy about his or her ability to create advertising messages, or even understanding why customers buy products. But such a broad statement in the face of billions of dollars of contrary evidence is hard to believe.

The number **7** reason for not advertising: **"I don't like your magazine."** Be it radio or magazines, television stations or billboards, every medium has an audience. The mechanism is to provide information, entertainment or common geography to gather together a group of individuals large enough to call an audience. Then sell access to the audience to companies that have products they wish to promote. The only thing that matters here is the color of the audience's money. If the money is green and plentiful, it more than fulfills the requirements of an advertiser. Advertisers don't need to like my product, like my readers or like much else other than my audience's propensity to purchase the advertisers products.

The number **6** reason for not advertising: **"I don't need any more business!"** This is really a great reason not to advertise, and at least the prospect understands the need to advertise. In my 30-plus years in the business, I have found this to be valid in only one instance. The advertising campaign we developed for the client was so successful; he had to stop soliciting more business so he could hire more employees to handle the increased business he was already getting. We actually switched his advertising budget from gaining more customers to recruiting new employees. And in the process of doing so, the recruitment message informed customers and prospects alike that this was a growing and successful business. We even asked current employees to be in the ads, which increased the morale of the entire company.

The number **5** reason for not advertising: **"I am not ready to advertise yet."** You know, every day someone buys something. Every day your competitor is attempting to woo away your customer. Every day is an opportunity to make a first impression with a new prospect. Waiting until you are ready is like waiting until you are totally out of debt to begin saving money. You will never get there.

The number **4** reason for not advertising: **"I tried advertising and it didn't work."** If advertising worked every time for everybody, nobody would be doing much of anything else. Like any discipline, it takes the best effort to generate results, and even then you are subject to myriad of influences outside of your control that could negate all of your hard work. Because so many people are advertising, it takes a good effort in order to generate results in the midst of the competition for consumer dollars. The alternative is to allow your business to grow or dwindle as a result of the market, without your taking any action to influence the market.

The number **3** reason for not advertising: **"You are too expensive."** If I've heard this once, I have heard it a thousand times. More often than not, my rates are very reasonable. I pride myself on having reasonable pricing for advertising. When I ask them, "relative to what?" I am usually told they are comparing my rates to a competitor. Now, all things being equal, I don't mind that comparison. But all things are never equal. Many competitors exaggerate about their circulation, and in some cases, actually quote space for less than it costs, which means there are lies in the equation someplace. There are some economic rules that cannot be violated, so I know this happens. I don't like to talk about my competitors, so that makes a discussion based upon comparison pretty hard to have. But the bottom line is that if an advertiser equates doing business with me in terms of "cost" and not as an investment, I have not done my job. As an investment, nobody cares how much the expenditure is, if the return from the investment justifies it.

The number **2** reason for not advertising: **"I need to talk to my … partner, wife, accountant, grandmother, etc."** It never fails to amaze me how a strong and decisive businessman can admit he must have another person's approval before he can make a decision to spend a few hundred bucks. These are the same executives that spend thousands to hire the right people, determine the direction of their companies over lunch, and usually have a travel and entertainment budget that rivals a Hollywood agent's. This person still needs to get the approval of someone else, who is always conveniently not available.

The number **1** reason for not advertising: **"My budget is spent."** This one is so good that 90 percent of my better customers use it today. The fact of the matter is that this reason is the most effective for getting rid of salespeople because so few salespeople understand the budgeting process. I know there is only about one account in a thousand who actually pays a full year in advance for their advertising expenditures. So what all the others are actually saying is that "my budget is allocated." They are not really saying that their budget is spent. In essence, the money has been earmarked for a specific use. The question for the prospect is this: "If your plan doesn't work, what are you going to do? Or, if your plan works so well that your sales goals are exceeded, how are you going to capitalize and continue to surpass your goals?" Both success and failure create reasons to advertise more, and possibly differently.

If these 10 reasons people use for not advertising or not advertising now, cause you to chuckle, imagine what they sound like to those of us who hear them all the time. Not many of them are close to being valid for a business who genuinely wishes to grow. They are given insincerely by people who fail to look a salesperson in the eye and say: "What you are proposing does not fit my plan," or "What you are asking me to buy is not that attractive to me." Salespeople deal fairly well with the truth. Too bad that prospects fear telling the truth and rely on obvious stalls like those listed above, rather than be forthcoming with salespeople.

The very best thing an advertising prospect can do is to tell the truth. If all businesses did so, it would force salespeople to create proposals that actually fit the potential clients' needs. The result would be that, eventually, all salespeople would be able to respond to customers' actual needs rather than listening to excuses that just don't hold up to scrutiny.

Back to some business basics

"Every man has his own destiny; the only imperative is to follow it, to accept it, no matter where it leads him."

— Henry Miller

What I love about business is that it is just common sense, and to be successful you just need to be able to understand the obvious. It's a good thing, because I'm not certain I could master anything really complicated. The first basic lesson of business is to bring in more money than goes out. Yes, there are times when you need to invest in product, promotion and/or customer development. But in the long run, business is about making more than you spend. Therefore sales must always be a prime focus.

Regardless of your sales paradigm, money coming in is the result of some form of sales. You may have a sales force, you may distribute through a system of wholesalers, or you sell directly to the consumer. If you are in business, you are in sales and all sales principles apply to you whether you embrace them or not.

The No. 2 basic business lesson is that there are only two ways to increase a company's profitability: increase revenues or decrease costs. More often than not a combination of the two is the course taken. You must understand that cutting costs can go only so far. Eventually, cutting back affects the quality of your product or service, and hence, will have a negative impact on your value equation, adversely affecting sales. Increasing revenues is one of the easiest ways to increase profitability. More money coming in the door gives you the opportunity to keep an increased portion of it. Even the best cost-cutting executive will admit it is impossible to keep any portion of income you have not made.

There are only two basic ways to increase revenues: Sell customers more product and/or services, or sell products and/or services to more customers. The first involves increasing the value of each transaction, and the second involves increasing the number of customers making transactions. In this day of Internet marketing, maximizing the value each acquired customer is accepted as the least expensive way to increase revenues. Acquiring new customers is, of course, the second way to increase revenues, but that is viewed as more expensive and sometimes more elusive than adding sales volume on your existing customers. Either way, additional dollars coming in through the door make it easier to keep a few as profit.

Advertising, although often misunderstood, works to sell more product as well as to garner more customers. Few advertisers are aware of the task they need their advertising to accomplish. If the task is clearly defined in their mind, the decisions that are necessary to execute the plan become more obvious. Case in point, if the advertiser wants to increase sales to current customers, the advertising needs to be focused within the media that the advertiser is currently using. The message should be consistent and the image should reflect much of what consumers already know about the product and/or service.

If the business wants to sell to additional (different) customers, then the advertising can be in the same and/or new media. The message should be new, and product features should be different from what has worked with other customers. The image can also be expanded or viewed from a different perspective, to make it acceptable to a different audience.

Customers are the lifeblood of a business. The third basic business lesson is to understand the value of your customer.

A close friend of mine, who was also an advertiser, used to argue with me that there is so much more security in being in business for your self than there is in working for someone else. He used to say that he could offend a quarter or even half of his customers and still have a job, whereas if I offended just one person (my boss), I could be easily unemployed. It was hard to argue with his logic. But he still did not have as good a grasp of the value of each customer as businesspeople should have today.

A customer buys your product and/or service. It is our hope that the customer will return and make additional purchases throughout the year. Many of our product offerings are intended to create just that scenario. The more transactions and the higher those transaction values, the more valuable is that customer. As an advertising medium, I am constantly telling my advertisers not to dwell on the single purchase a new customer from my magazine makes, but to look at each new customer in terms of lifetime value.

We recently had an advertiser utilize our e-newsletters to advertise a specific product. Once customers clicked on the advertiser's banner ad they were asked to buy a specific product. But out of 1,700 click-throughs only a few subscribers bought the offering. These purchases were not enough to justify the expense in the advertiser's mind. However, if in addition to the specific product offering, the advertiser would have promised a free premium in return for the name and e-mail address of the click-through, and then calculated the potential lifetime value of all 1,700 click-throughs, millions of dollars would have been running through his head. As it is, looking for the one-time sale resulted in a lost opportunity.

Just one more thing about this example, 1,700 is roughly the number of people it takes to fill 29 Greyhound buses. Imagine having 29 Greyhound buses drive up to your business! All of those people walk through your front door, and yet you are not prepared to make sales to any more than a handful of that number. Wouldn't you feel as if you had missed a great opportunity?

Common sense sometimes means being able to see the benefit that comes to us, even though we weren't seeking it. You must be aware that success does not always have the appearance that we expect. We cannot afford to become so focused on getting a specific result that we miss a benefit that may surpass our original goal. There are many days when the stars are aligned in our favor, yet we fail to see them because we are narrowly focused or looking the other way.

Look at successful companies. They do not do things that fail to work. They do not routinely waste money. They could not continue in business employing poor practices. They constantly try to cut their costs. So should you. They are always increasing their revenues. So should you. They sell customers more product and/or services. So should you. They sell products and/or services to more customers. So should you. They advertise to do so. So should you.

I am always amazed at how small-business people often believe their businesses can survive without advertising when giants like Coca Cola, Chase Bank, General Motors, etc.; know that they cannot survive without it. It is just common sense, watching what successful businesses do and then doing those same things ourselves. The next time you are thinking of doing something you perceive is extraordinary, stop and ask yourself, would Coca Cola cancel their entire advertising budget in a pinch? Would Chase Bank stop selling credit cards for the remainder of the year? Would General Motors not come out with next year's model in order to save money? If your answer is the obvious one, then maybe your decision is not the right one to make. Remember these large companies have remarkable common sense and business savvy. Maybe, just maybe, we could learn from following their lead and using our own common sense.

AIDA

"The big print giveth and the small print taketh away."

— Tom Waitts

I have written about the specific steps in the advertising process before, but the fundamental steps of advertising are so often misunderstood, I thought it best to revisit the subject from my perspective as a consumer. And in the process, I get to share a great experience.

The acronym AIDA stands for Attention, Interest, Desire and Action, which are the four specific steps that advertising should achieve to effectively sell a company's products. These distinctions are achieved before any product is sold, whether they are attained intentionally or accidentally.

I am a big Jack Nicholson fan. I can't imagine a bigger thrill in life than being able to meet that man. So when I first saw the trailer for a new film with Nicholson and Morgan Freeman, I stopped what I was doing to find out more. I know Nicholson and Freeman are both great at comedy and drama, but I wondered how the two would work together. Just their names got my Attention.

To sell something you must fulfill a real or perceived need. A common strategy is to lead with conflict, that is, a problem that is familiar to your target audience. Surprisingly, the human condition is such that we all take our problems very personally, believing that few others suffer the same way or with the same intensity as we ourselves do. Truth be known, we all feel pretty much the same way about most things. Annoyances are a constant for all of us. This fact provides marketers with an almost universal opportunity to get our Interest by getting us to identify with the conflict.

The Bucket List, as Morgan Freeman's character explains to Jack Nicholson's, is a list of those things you want to accomplish in life before you kick the bucket. Wow! For a 50-something-year-old that grew up with ambitious dreams and made compromises with life as time went on, the concept really got me thinking. When I was young and idealistic, I remember the sadness I felt the first time I compromised a dream for the reality of providing for my family. It was not a hard decision because I love my family. But it was the beginning of a succession of choices that replaced my visions of greatness with the need to be reliable and dependable.

I have more than a passive Interest in the concept of recapturing those lofty goals that I willingly exchanged for a life shared with others. The melancholy I feel when I think of those abandoned dreams is embarrassing as it brings tears so close to the surface; I fear someone might see them or hear my voice quiver as I speak. Maybe like our other human conditions, this isn't only my response, but a universal reaction to unfulfilled ambitions.

Attention and Interest, if well conceived, can only lead to Desire. As I put my life into the scenario of this movie, I knew seeing it would satisfy a longing in me that has been unfulfilled for a while.

The movie studio did a perfect job of hooking me. Each time I saw a trailer during the initial days of the promotion, a little bit more of the plotline was revealed. I knew the movie was going to be about two guys who were engaged in doing those really outrageous and memorable things that they gave up at an earlier age. I knew I would enjoy it, too, if only vicariously, by watching the movie. I really wanted to see this film.

I determined to ask my wife if she'd like to see this film too. The next time the trailer came on TV, my wife was in the room, and before I could say a word, she said, "Let's go see that movie." Funny how quickly decisions can be made when you are not analyzing the individual steps that go into the process leading to a decision.

The Action step to attend this film took the form of one of our "dates." We went out for a nice lunch and then to see the film. Each step of the AIDA process was part of this purchase decision. The marketer used emotional triggers to stimulate my purchase.

I actually enjoy being sold. I like it when a marketer takes the time to get my Attention with a product. I am satisfied when they use the product benefits to flirt with me and get my Interest. I get anxious when they finally persuade me to the point that I desire the product, and they find the final button to push that causes me to Act and make a purchase. Most times I am happy with the process. When it is done well, I am actually a little proud to have been sold. As much as I have been manipulated, I have no regrets, nor do I feel that I lack a free choice.

The Bucket List? It was very satisfying movie with Jack Nicholson at his best. And I highly recommend not only the concept of making your own bucket list (my wife and I are making one together), but also seeing the movie. The film makes you feel good about life. Without giving away the plotline, you do get to vicariously fulfill some of those dreams which many of us have given up on. The movie will make you laugh and eventually will make you cry. And when Jack Nicholson's character completes his list by finally kissing the most beautiful girl in the world (the granddaughter he did not know he had), you will realize how lucky each and every one of us really are.

"Patience? I'm going to kill something!"

"Contrary to what self-appointed protectors of the consumer so loudly proclaim, advertising does not cause people to buy bad products. Nothing will put a bad product out of business faster than a good advertising campaign. Advertising causes people to try a product once, but poor quality eliminates any possibility of a repeat purpose."

— Morris Hite

Sales, especially, advertising sales is not a passive vocation. We do not sit back and wait for customers to come to us. If you look in the dictionary under self-starter you may well see the picture of an advertising salesperson. I learned early in my career that we are a unique breed and that the rest of the world often observes us with a healthy dose of suspicion. We move just a little bit too fast for those not attuned to our world.

After a few years of selling radio advertising in the small market of Bloomington, Ind., I was offered a job by the second-ranked station in Indianapolis. During the interview, I was shown a drawing of the station's mascot—a buzzard. It seems the station was built upon the cartoon of two buzzards sitting on a high-tension wire overlooking a chicken farm. One buzzard looks at the other and says, "Patience? I'm going to kill something!" The station was owned by Fairbanks Broadcasting and run by an outstanding broadcaster and CEO, Jim Hilliard, with advertising sales handled by VP of Sales, Dick Yancey. As a company we had no patience for waiting to see what might happen. We were determined to make things happen and became experts at doing just that.

Our sister station was No. 1 in the market and we were No. 2. We dominated the radio market and were determined never to relinquish the lead. We took market leadership seriously and did what the market leader should do. We always took the high road when faced with a tactic from a competitor who challenged our position. It would have been easier to use the same negative tactics to fend off these challenges, but we considered ourselves above that. So we worked harder, smarter and with more determination to win.

Aside from the daily association with a most-professional group of broadcasters, working for and later with Dick Yancey was an extraordinary experience. Never did a day start without Yancey asking us if we were having fun. He wouldn't accept anything else. Because, as he would say, if you aren't having fun doing this you should find something else to do. There are too many other things that are fun and pay pretty good money to be miserable doing a job this hard. If you passed the first question, he'd smile at you, wink and say, "Let's go kill something," referring to the cartoon that we adopted as our mission statement.

In addition to honing my sales skills, Dick Yancey taught me about human nature. He always asked why people did this or why they did that. Understanding why they did or didn't do something was more important that understanding what they were going to do. He was very insightful when it came to the customer's buying motivations. He immediately saw the business reasons, professional reasons and personal reasons that would motivate a customer to buy a product. He taught me how to intuitively address all three motives simultaneously in the sales process. He inspired those of us who sold for him to challenge ourselves to be better each day. He never used fear or scarcity to motivate us. He showed respect for us and expected us to be the best in the market. Our pride made sure none of us would dare let him down.

Dick believed that repeat sales came not from a good product, but ultimately from a happy customer. And he believed that there were many ways beyond product to keep a customer happy. He taught us how much more a good salesman impacted sales than a good product.

Today, customers have a very good grasp of the products we sell. The vast amount of information available from the Internet alone has created a culture where the buyer knows as much and sometimes more about the product than the seller. It's true that buyers are not always armed with the correct information, but it is true that they have access to much more information than they need to make a decision. So how do they decide between products of equally perceived value? They buy the one represented by the salesperson or company that makes them happy. Unfortunately, it could default to the salesperson or company that offends them the least. Is that something you think about? I know you don't want to offend your customers, but do you take the time to think about actually making your customers happy?

Most companies do not. Like athletic teams who fight aggressively through most of a game to get a lead, and then play the remaining period not to lose rather than fighting to win, most businesses defend what they have rather than create what they want. Taking your customer from satisfied to happy is not as directly connected to the bottom line as turning a prospective customer into a new customer. Most companies will not invest to make the next step. I learned in the early days of my sales career that a happy customer will see you through good times and bad. A customer that buys your product because you are the least-objectionable option will be gone at the drop of a hat. Selling the least-objectionable product is like playing not to lose.

My years at Fairbanks were really fun and exciting. Not only did we enjoy what we did, we were good at it, and we were always determined to win. And we won at virtually everything we attempted. Creating a culture for winning was not that hard to do. Sales-savvy Hilliard and Yancey, along with sales managers Tim Medland and Bill Johnson, found us winning almost daily. We were always celebrating a win at something. They routinely put us into situations where we could not lose, and then reinforced every win, even if the victory did not live up to expectations. The obsession of finding the win in virtually every initiative became as important as the initiative. Being acknowledged and celebrated daily as a winner has an amazing affect on a person, but an even more amazing affect on a company and its culture.

Teach your employees to make your customers happy because a happy customer buys more than a satisfied customer. Keep your employees happy because happy employees are productive employees. Fun is profitable. Tell me, have you ever seen an employee with a frown setting productivity records? Yet too often we push for increased productivity and never connect productivity to the enjoyment our employees derive from their job. Find a company with high customer satisfaction as well as high productivity, and you won't find many unhappy employees. Is that a coincidence? I don't think so.

Create an atmosphere of winning. Find wins in every situation that you can because even minor wins are addictive. The more an employee wins, the more they will do to continue winning. The addiction to winning for empowered employees creates a positive culture every bit as much as the habit of losing breeds boredom and disempowered employees.

That extraordinary winning team from Fairbanks Broadcasting split up, and we went our separate ways not long after the company was sold to Blair Broadcasting in 1984. All of those former co-workers, that I have kept track of, have done well in their careers. Yet none of us have found an environment as rich in "can do" attitude as the one we created and enjoyed together.

I learned from those days that you could recognize a company filled with a winning attitude when you walked in the front door. The atmosphere would be filled with excitement and anticipation. Similarly, you could feel the pending depression and disappointment in the air when you walked through the door of a company on the rocks. It is the bored and disempowered employee that says, "Have patience," and the empowered employee determined to be a winner who says, "Patience. Hell! I'm going to kill something."

The Image Makers

"The business community wants remarkable advertising, but turns a cold shoulder to the kind of people who can produce it. That is why most advertisements are so infernally dull.... our business needs massive transfusions of talent. And talent, I believe, is most likely to be found among nonconformists, dissenters, and rebels."

— David Ogilvy

When I sense trouble or uncertainty in the future, I often look to the past for guidance. For it is true that if you do not learn from history you are often doomed to repeat it. Such is the case as I write this chapter of ADvice. With the recent events surrounding our economy and Wall Street, an air of uncertainty covers us all.

Looking back into the history of American business, I began reading the history of Ray Kroc, the man behind the rise of the fast-food giant McDonald's, to gain some inspiration. I wanted to be able to write something that gave a strong sense of hope for the future and was not just echoes of the gloom and doom espoused by the evening news concerning today's market.

I learned that Ray Kroc as a young man joined the Red Cross to train as a driver, along with another icon in American history, Walt Disney. The war ended before Kroc completed his training, so he was not sent overseas, but Walt Disney and Ray Kroc continued as lifelong friends after their service together in the World War I era.

Kroc's love was playing the piano, a career he religiously pursued after the war, until he could no longer pay his bills. He was forced to take a job selling restaurant supplies. He was moderately successful doing this. Then in 1937 he ran across a company that sold milk-shake mixers; he paid $10,000 for the domestic sales rights for the Prince Castle Multimixer. By 1940 he had amassed a small fortune from the sale of these machines to soda fountains and restaurants across the country. It was then that he ran into Richard and Maurice McDonald, whose new and unique approach to selling food was creating a stir in California.

Most know the story after that. Kroc arranged to franchise the restaurant concept started by Richard and Maurice McDonald, amassing a tremendous fortune as golden arches were built across the entire country over the next 30 years. As much as I hate to admit it, advertising for McDonald's during this period was more or less an afterthought. It was truly a "build it and they will come," era for the company. America's love affair with fast food and uniform production standards of food service fueled unprecedented growth.

During the same time, in his hometown of Berne, Ind., there was a family—a husband, wife and two sons—named Reinhard. The father, who worked at one of the local furniture companies as an upholsterer, died from complications of the flu in 1939. The mother, Agnes, was forced to work as a cashier in the local grocery store in order to supplement the $92 the family received each month from the government. The eldest of the two boys, Keith, began working four years later at the age of 8 to help support the family.

Keith worked after school pulling weeds and doing various other things to help his family. Since his mother worked, Keith got a good deal of support from his grandparents who lived nearby. In Berne, being a small Swiss Mennonite community, the church was central to the culture. It was there that Keith spent much of his growing-up time.

Keith could not afford college so he continued to work, and after high school, he became a photographer's assistant, learning the craft which propelled him into becoming a commercial artist. By 1963 Keith Reinhart, then 28, was married with two children and working at the Biddle Agency in Bloomington, Ill. His first break came as he was asked to work on an advertising campaign for an insurance company. Pulling from his childhood experience when the loss of his father resulted in such hardship, and having witnessed his mother be treated poorly at the hands of an insurance company over his father's insurance policy, he knew exactly the image that would serve his client. In addition to a series of ads portraying the insurance company helping its policyholders he created a song that summed up the message: "Like a good neighbor, State Farm is there." His campaign changed the insensitive image of State Farm Insurance into one of a caring company.

In 1964 after winning several awards, Keith Reinhard was recruited to the Chicago advertising agency of Needham, Louis & Brorby which became Needham, Harper & Steers the next year.

At the same time Reinhard's career was taking off, the growth of Ray Kroc's burger empire was slowing. There were other fast-food restaurants and the glow of fast food itself was beginning to dim. The golden arches could be seen in most major cities across the country. Still living on the "build it and they will come," marketing approach, McDonald's was not enjoying the popularity that it had become accustomed to having. So finally, in 1970, Ray Kroc decided to turn to advertising to revitalize his business. He committed to increasing his advertising budget and hiring a new and more creative advertising agency.

Kroc took the McDonald's account to New York's Madison Avenue, the self-acclaimed center of advertising creativity. Shop after shop pitched the McDonald's account with campaigns espousing the great taste of McDonald's hamburgers and fries.

Meanwhile in Chicago, Keith Reinhard took his wife and kids to McDonald's several times. He immediately realized how the experience brightened the day of his family. He interviewed patrons and confirmed that experienced was not isolated to his family. He conducted hamburger taste tests with hundreds of consumers and discovered that there was no discernable difference between a McDonald's hamburger and those of the competition. He needed to create a campaign, not based upon the food, which his research pointed out was indistinguishable from the rest. He needed a campaign based upon the dining experience.

Reinhard took all of his research and found the voice, the slogan and the image to bring Middle America back to McDonald's. The five words, "You Deserve a Break Today," and the accompanying advertising campaign did more to revitalize the ailing burger giant than anything in its history. Several years later in 1975, as the advertising industry goes, McDonald's tired of the "You Deserve a Break Today" campaign and sought something new. Again Reinhard's Needham, Harper & Steers delivered with "You, You're the one."

In 1981, Reinhard's firm finally did lose the McDonald's account to the Leo Burnett Agency. But determined to succeed, Keith Reinhard's business grew nearly as much and as fast as McDonald's. In 1986, as CEO of Needham, Harper & Steers, Reinhard orchestrated the merger of Needham, Harper & Steers with Doyle, Dane, Bernbach (DDB) to form the largest advertising holding company in the world, Omnicom. And finally, as DDB Needham Worldwide celebrated its 50th anniversary in 1998, McDonald's again awarded its account to Reinhard's company.

Not bad for a boy from the Swiss Mennonite community of Berne, Ind.

Reading a history of advertising, makes me realize that even though today may be tough, it is just one of thousands of days in an advertising career. There will undoubtedly be more tough days, but there are also going to be many more good ones. And if I hang around and consistently give my best, there occasionally will be those days that are spectacular, days that define a career. Keep it in mind because I am sure the same will be available for you.

Thanks to Keith Reinhard for the inspiration, from another guy who worked in Berne, IN.

Training & Development

"It takes a big idea to attract the attention of consumers and get them to buy your product. Unless your advertising contains a big idea, it will pass like a ship in the night. I doubt if more than one campaign in a hundred contains a big idea."

— David Ogilvy

Over the years, I have trained and managed in excess of 170 employees in sales positions. I started to say that I have trained and managed in excess of 170 salespeople, but that would not be accurate. Being in a sales position does not make someone a salesperson, just as having a job as a teacher does not automatically make someone a good educator. Unfortunately, the occupation of salesperson in general has an image that is not conducive to being viewed as a profession; that is, it is not seen as a career that requires considerable training and specialized study. That view is erroneous.

Sales as a profession, is very hard. Far too many people misunderstand the vast set of skills one must master in order to achieve competence in the selling arena. Like a trial attorney, the true sales professional usually will not ask any questions to which he or she doesn't already know the answers. Salespeople approach conversations like playing chess, anticipating the prospect's next three, four or five responses, and the direction those responses will take the conversation. Some employees in sales positions think because they can talk, they can sell. Nothing is further from the truth

The most difficult aspect of training salespeople is to help them discover that they actually need training. A key ingredient of a salesperson's makeup is self-esteem. This characteristic is required so that salespeople can withstand rejection as often as they surely will, and so that they will not allow the rejection to reflect personally upon themselves. But healthy self-esteem also prevents many from being aware that they actually need training. How do you tell someone that they are a failure at a skill they don't even know exists?

Creating an atmosphere where a salesperson can become aware of what they don't know that they don't know is by far my biggest challenge as a manager. Until a person is aware that something is missing, he will always feel that he is complete.

In many sports, and some business situations, you may have heard the term "in the zone." You might be able to imagine a concept, but to totally understand the distinction between the concept and the reality requires you to actually be "in the zone" and experience the feeling. It's kind of like the distinction of balance that you experience when you are learning to ride a bicycle. Until you learn the knack of maintaining balance, you can observe how to do it, and can almost imagine yourself doing it, but you still fall down. Once you get the distinction, you understand balance from an entirely new perspective. You can actually practice balance and improve on it, which not only increases your ability to ride a bicycle well, but also impacts a multitude of other functions.

During this very difficult period for those wishing to learn sales, I have learned not to impose my will or to bestow my thoughts upon novice sales types. Many of them, especially a high percentage of today's younger generation entering the workforce, are colored by a sense of entitlement. While I watch these folks in what I call their unconsciously incompetent period, it is best to wait until they become frustrated and eventually ask for help. They seldom take advice or guidance until they hit the wall; that's when they consider the possibility that there may be a few things they don't know. This is the most difficult period in training and development. It requires a lot of patience on my part. At times I feel as if I am the only one that can see these things, and the rest of those around me live in blissful ignorance.

Early in my career, I jumped in too soon and offered the benefit of my knowledge. My help was not welcomed, and it was met by employees who either considered me out of touch with things or too narrow in my observations of the current situation. I am still amazed at how wise a person with six months of sales experience is compared to the 35 years I have.

When the unconscious sales employee becomes conscious of their incompetence, the fun really begins. This is the part of training that I really enjoy because once the admission comes that there might be something more to know, the employee becomes a student anxious to learn. They now know there is something missing, and as long as they attempt to fill the void, they will ask for and voraciously consume help and new concepts. They are now consciously incompetent and will do most anything to become competent by filling in the void. As they discover what they need to learn, and how they need to practice to become proficient, it is fun watching them make progress.

The first step in moving from consciously incompetent to consciously competent is to notice the moment. Asking a salesperson to pay attention is one of the most difficult things there is to do. As I said earlier, most employees in a sales position believe that because they can talk, then they can sell. Well, to pay attention you must listen, which is a particularly hard thing to do when you are talking too! But as hard as it is, those who become truly frustrated by not selling actually become pretty good at listening. When they become a consistent listener and practice it with a passion, they become salespeople who sell on purpose in a remarkably short period of time.

It is not in vogue to be a Bob Knight fan these days as much as it was in the 1970s and '80s. But I am a fan and have been since the early '70s. Coach Knight has a unique perspective on becoming a champion that I happen to share. While at Indiana University, Coach Knight was asked about his team, and their desire to win. He responded (and I am paraphrasing), "The desire to win is no big deal. About anyone who competes in any area has the desire to win to one degree or another. But the desire to prepare to win is what is unusual. Those few who are willing to prepare, and who work like everything is on the line during the practice session, and who give it their all in preparation so they will be prepared when the moment of truth comes, that is what is unusual, and that is what makes a champion."

What Coach Knight was talking about is working at becoming unconsciously competent. Practice your skill set and perfect it, until it becomes automatic, becoming so adept that you no longer need to think about it.

The goal of training and development is to go from unconsciously incompetent to consciously incompetent to consciously competent and finally to unconsciously competent. In terms of difficulty, you can imagine pushing a boulder to the top of a mountain as the first step. The second step is rolling the boulder over a flat but long plateau. Steps three and four compare to rolling the boulder down the other side of the mountain.

There is more to the sales profession than just being a good listener. But listening is as good a trait as any to explain the difficulty in training someone in a skill they are not consciously aware exists. And of course, this process is not just a one-time thing with salespeople. There are dozens of distinctions a true professional salesperson must learn. I face frustration with senior salespeople as much as with new ones. Sometimes those who have gone through the process a couple of times are the hardest ones to convince there is more to learn. Each and every time you must approach your pupil understanding that they believe they know everything there is to know. I have been learning how to sell for over 35 years, and as reluctantly as those I train, I find I still have much to learn.

The evolution of retailing

Many years ago, I owned a merchandising support company, Impulse Broadcast Systems (IBS). We provided in-store music systems integrated with audio commercials that were synchronized to individual store merchandising sets. Our company was one of the first to use satellite technology and digitized audio from computer hard drives. It was pretty high tech stuff for 1991.

IBS is where I learned a lot about mass merchandising, especially the grocery industry. As I grew up in central Indiana, like everyone else I visited the local grocery store with my family. In the 60s, most grocery stores had a large meat freezer in the back of the store. There were generally one or more large store rooms surrounding the consumer shopping area of the store.

In the early part of the decade the grocery industry was the classic "push" sales model. The manufacturer's salesman would visit the grocery store and sell cake mix. The salesman might sell a railroad train carload of a name-brand cake mix to the store owner, offering to give a discount and carry the financing of the order for immediate delivery. The grocer would thus fill the store shelves and much of the storage area around the store. The grocer in nearly every case was not aware of how long it would take to sell a carload of cake mix.

In the early 60s, the employees stocking shelves knew more about the grocery store's inventory than the owner or manager. But that was about to change.

About the same time, a student working on his doctoral thesis at the University of Chicago was perfecting a system of cataloging using a series of lines and corresponding numbers. This student was addressing the problem of a creating common system of product identification.

In Dayton, Ohio the relatively small National Cash Register Company was experimenting with broader uses of new technology being developed by NASA in hopes of creating new products to lead the company forward in the next decade. Their work with lasers was beginning to make progress.

And computer systems, which in 1960 filled rooms, were becoming smaller and cheaper. The prospect of smaller companies owning a computer was in the foreseeable future.

These seemingly-unrelated situations collided in the mid 60s, when the Marsh grocery chain in Yorktown, Indiana was facing a possible strike by employees. Employees like Jack Williams who stocked shelves for the grocer. Jack and his colleagues knew how much sold and how much to re-order when the time came. The specter of these employees unionizing upset the owners because they realized that those very employees effectively carried the company's inventory management system in their heads. Management knew they were in a weak negotiating position.

Driven by Marsh, NCR pushed laser scanning technology in conjunction with the development of the uniform product code system to track product sales at the point of purchase in grocery stores and created UPC scanning systems. The payoff was not the avoidance of hiring skilled unionized cash register operators, as many surmised, but the development of immediately useful sales data and management information systems. MIS allowed the grocer to know just how many boxes of cake mix he sold every hour of every day.

As a result, the grocer now could tell the cake mix salesman that he didn't want to buy and store a railroad car load of cake mixes. He was only going to buy 23 boxes of chocolate cake mix to be delivered Monday morning at 9, then another 17 boxes to be delivered Tuesday morning at 9. This knowledge led to "just-in-time" inventory systems and forced an elaborate "pull" sales technology to be employed by manufacturers.

Grocers no longer wanted excess stock and hence had no reason to have large storage areas surrounding their stores. The back room and storage areas were converted to the bakery, a larger produce section, a delicatessen, a floral shop, and other departments selling highly perishable products that could now be profitable with an accurate product sales forecast. Small grocery stores now became supermarkets with multiple departments on the periphery of the main stocking area. Packaged good manufacturers were, for the first time, in step with consumer purchasing. Store owners no longer would buy big orders because they received a discount or credit. The only way for manufacturers to sell more was to stimulate consumers to buy more, creating a sales velocity "pull" for their product through the distribution chain.

Many companies fell by the wayside as retailing evolved. These companies failed to see the opportunity to increase sales by advertising directly to the consumer. After all, they reasoned, it was the grocer's responsibility to advertise to his own customer. These companies reasoned that they were just a supplier. But they failed to realize that grocers were now buying product according to how fast the consumer purchased the product. Inventory mix was now dictated by consumer purchasing, which was impacted by consumer advertising. These retail stores were now being managed as real estate operations generating dollars per square inch, and how many times the inventory turned per square inch: the faster the turnover, the higher the profits. Discounts in price could no longer compete with the profitability of fast product turnover and consumer "pull."

Advertising budgets split into branding and product promotion. The age of the discount coupon began. Consumer promotion, i.e., ways to motivate the consumer to buy, became the manufacturer's way to sell more product. Finding additional uses for products and advertising those new uses fueled incremental sales for established items.

Supermarkets were now just a conduit between the producer and the consumer. MIS systems could tell the grocer not only how much of each product would sell, but which days it would sell. Expensive computer modeling programs tracked such things as the impact of a 10% discount, temporary price reductions (TPRs), weekly ad placements, off-shelf displays, items stocked in the aisles and on endcaps, and the funds spent by manufacturers to tell consumers where to find their products. Each function, and every combination of functions, affects product sales levels. The results are constantly changing, influenced by weather, the seasons, and geography.

Before computerization, grocers selected a product mix and sold to loyal customers. Manufacturers now compete to buy distribution, provide just-in-time delivery, and secure prime eye-level shelf space in aisles and on endcaps. They purchase newspaper promotions to ensure their products get added impact. They negotiate TPRs, provide proven consumer promotion and assume the risk of not having their product restocked if it doesn't achieve sales velocity or adequate turnover. All because Jack Williams, the stock boy at Marsh grocery store knew his job better than his manager and he wanted a raise.

Grocery retailing is highly competitive and much more sophisticated than most realize. But it provides lessons for those in other industries. With strong sales information from MIS software, retailers will only carry products with high product turnover or velocity. This information will in essence turn retailers into companies leasing real estate by the square inch. Velocity or product turnover will be measured by dollars per square inch per day. Retailers will not carry products that do not sell quickly. And eventually they will only carry products with bona fide consumer promotion (advertising) behind them that insure consumers know where and why they need to buy the product. Even demand-products, i.e., the selection of products that nearly everyone buys on each grocery trip (eggs, orange juice, coffee, bread, milk, lettuce, and bananas) will need consumer promotion in order to consistently secure shelf space with progressive retailers.

The four questions

"The simplest definition of advertising, and one that will probably meet the test of critical examination, is that advertising is selling in print."

— Daniel Starch

When I sold advertising, I wanted to be the best ad salesperson I could be. I discovered that just about everyone who bought advertising had some questions. Since these questions addressed advertising accountability, most of my colleagues avoided answering them, not because they didn't want to, but because they didn't know how to answer them.

In order to set myself apart from ordinary ad salespeople, I studied advertising and developed strategies that led me to be confident that I could provide solid answers. In spite of the fact that I was one of the very few willing to accept responsibility for this accountability, many advertisers still found it difficult to meet my conditions for being accountable for their results.

What every advertiser wants to know, whether they express it in these words or not, is:

- How much will my business grow using what you are proposing?
- How much will this growth cost me?
- How long will it take to achieve this growth?
- How will I know that your program caused this growth?

These are hard questions that speak directly to advertising accountability. Most advertisers will not accept direct accountability for their own efforts when they control the total advertising budget, so you can see how confrontational the questions might be to someone selling media.

Being able to take responsibility for a business's growth begins with a complete understanding of how and where they have advertised in the past, as well as their customer metrics.

Here's a real life example: The Example Company has sales of $5,325,000 per year with an advertising budget of $213,000. This is 4% of sales. The company had 11,501 transactions last year with an average transaction of $463.00. from 2,175 different customers. Their average customer had 5.29 transactions and spent $2,448.28.

Knowing these metrics makes it relatively easy to forecast growth. The first step is to establish a budget to maintain existing business. If it took $213,000 to generate $5,325,000 in sales last year, why would take any less to do it this year?

Next, estimate/establish a viable growth percentage, such as 5%, or $266,000, as an objective. Knowing the client's average order is $463.00 means we would have to generate about 575 new average orders. At 5.29 orders per customer, it also means they would need 108.7 new customers, IF these customers all started in the first month or so. Assuming they can add new customers equally through out the year, they need to reach 108.7 new customers at the end of six months (an annualized new customer rate of 217.4) to achieve an average growth rate of 575 new average transactions per year. Last year, the company spent $213,000, or $97.93 per customer, to serve a customer base of 2, 175. They will need to spend an additional $21,290.00 ($97.93 times 217.4) targeted at non-customers whose profile matches our existing customers.

It is interesting to note that many would target growth of just 108.7 new customers for the year. Since these new customers come on board at a rate of 9.06 new customers per month, their accumulated customer base at mid-year would be 54.34 new customers, which would generate only half the sales needed to reach the sales goal. At this rate, the number of customers needed to generate the targeted sales revenues would be reached only in the last month. This is the main reason advertising investment needed for growth should always be double the dollars spent to maintain existing customers.

Too many companies fail to realize the cost of growth. Even then, they fail to realize how expensive it can be to re-establish a growth model after just a few months of cutting back. Unfortunately, most companies develop structures too small for the growth they want, rather than structuring adequately to achieve it. Not only do they fail to use the correct mathematical formulas, but they also fail to have contingency plans in case other factors impact their strategies.

Understanding these metrics makes answering the first three questions easier. Answering the last question is generally a matter of tracking results on at least a monthly - if not weekly - basis. Again, this comes back to identifying who are existing customers and knowing when you get new customers. Additionally, a continual check on average transaction value is needed in order to know that promotional discounts are not eroding new ground gained by cutting margins.

If you find an advertising person willing to work with you in terms of your transactions, average order and customer count, you have found someone who can honestly help your business grow. You will need to share detailed sales metrics and strategy so they can help your business grow.

Another way to grow your business consists of increasing your average transaction. This can be achieved by advertising additional uses for your products to your existing customers, adding compatible product lines for existing customers, and/or developing and selling products that are consumed at a faster rate than your current products. Any combination can increase your average transaction.

Back to the four questions, if you are lucky enough to find someone who will accept accountability for one of these questions, you are way ahead of the game. If you find someone willing to accept accountability for more than one, make sure you develop a solid, long-term relationship with that person.

I spent many years learning how to answer these four questions. These days, I seldom go through the exercise and share the answers with others. I find few people are willing to earn success from advertising as we know it should happen. Too many expect results beyond what their efforts or investments actually merit.

As a friend of mine put it, "Instant gratification is no longer fast enough." This is the attitude that keeps advertising a mystery. The failure to accept the correlation of what you put in to what you get out is why so few people understand advertising. Everyone expects to receive more than reality is ready to deliver. And advertising is more often blamed than the erroneous expectations of misinformed people.

Trumped

"If you will call your troubles experiences, and remember that every experience develops some latent force within you, you will grow vigorous and happy, however adverse your circumstances may seem to be."

— John R. Miller

What do I have in common with Donald Trump? Not much. He has extensive real estate holdings. He still has most of his hair. My mode of transportation is not nearly as glamorous. And, in my apprentice program, "You're fired/hired!" is not the climax.

Over the years, I have shared a lot of advertising concepts and ideas. Those I have given some of my best material often cannot get past the thought that I had something to gain from helping them. It seems that the less that was in it for me, the more resistance my ideas and concepts met. I guess people fear a hidden agenda on my part, when none exists other than my honest desire to be helpful.

A few months ago I mentioned to my sales manager, how I would like to take a business and make them famous. The reason was to give my staff to have an irrefutable case study on the power of advertising. You see, the majority of advertising salespeople do not know how effective advertising can be. They are so busy selling ad space and concepts that they have not taken the time to learn how advertising works. Too many salespeople ask advertisers to spend money with only the hope that it will work. They feel woefully ignorant about what strategies advertisers should use.

My philosophy has always been this: if we, as purveyors of ad space, don't know the best and most effective ways to use our medium, who will? More importantly, how can we with a clear conscience recommend that an advertiser buy a specific package or campaign without the knowledge of what works? Those salespeople who don't know how to make their medium work actually believe that advertisers who are not familiar with their medium actually know better how to make it work. That's like believing my father can drive a race car because he attends NASCAR races.

If you are like me, you do not want to look stupid. When I buy an unfamiliar product, I ask the salesman some basic questions. I do so to support my conviction that I am doing the right thing. The difference between speaking to someone who knows their product versus someone who is 'selling me' is obvious. The person who knows how and why their product works has an innate confidence that makes me feel like I am in good company. The salesperson just selling me leaves me feeling as if my money is the only thing he is interested in. Even the best salesmanship skills cannot mask the difference.

I do not want those representing our company to be from the latter group. I want our company represented by those who instill confidence in our customer's decision to purchase.

Several weeks ago, I received an email in response to an earlier chapter of ADvice suggesting that I give specific input and advice to the sender to help their business. It was not a request for charity, but a plea for expertise from a business wishing to grow to the point where it could and would continue advertising on its own. This email set into motion a series of events. I receive far too many requests and/or demands that I give something free to a profit-generating company as if it is my responsibility to subvert my profitability because someone else wants me to do so. I frequently hear how my product is not worth what I ask for it because someone in another business has an "opinion" about the value of my product. (You know, I have opinions about their products too!)

For one reason or another, this plea was different and hit me on a day when I was in the right frame of mind to do something about it. You see, I also have another philosophy in life. People like to complain. I do too. I love to moan and groan about all sorts of things. It makes conversation interesting from time to time when you can point to the shortcomings of other people or situations. Part of my thought process is this: If God blessed you with the ability to see those shortcomings and you wish to entertain yourself and others by complaining about them, you have an inherent responsibility to do something about them. So I am -- I am putting up rather than shutting up.

I complain about advertisers doing the wrong thing. I complain about advertisers being fearful of committing to an advertising plan when things are tight. I complain that advertisers spend too little, or quit, before the tide is about turn and make it begin to pay off. It's easy for me to do, because it's not my money. It's easy for me to do, because I can go on to the next business. It's easy for me to do, because I don't have a vested interest in your success. It was easy for me to do until now.

Last month at our annual advertising sales summit, I divided the eight salespeople and four support staff into two equal teams. The teams were each assigned a business selected by my sales manager and me. The businesses are young companies with limited resources who have agreed to work exclusively with these teams on their marketing and advertising functions for a year. Teams were given identical amounts of resources: ad space, graphic art, and online exposure. The teams are competing to see who can make the company they are representing the most effective and well-known in the next year.

Much like Donald Trump's The Apprentice, these teams will create initiatives for the growth of these businesses. The teams will compete in the real marketplace representing real companies and real products, putting their expertise and skill on the line to grow the sales of two relatively-new ventures. Diane and I will routinely meet with the teams to monitor their progress and make sure that we build a comprehensive case study for other new businesses to follow.

I'll be honest: we are not being altruistic about this. My staff will benefit greatly from this effort. The experience is bound to educate my staff beyond most advertising salespeople. I expect it make a big difference to those considering my company versus other companies. I believe advertisers like you would rather work with salespeople who know what they are doing because they have been there and have made the tough decisions you faced every day.

I can't identify the two companies because I do not want affect the outcome of this case study. Each person on my staff will learn exactly what it takes to become effective in our publications. My staff will, by necessity, learn the dynamics of small businesses that affect their ability to compete in our industry. At the end of the period, I will have two case studies that we can use as models for other business. And, even though I won't say, "You're fired/hired," I will not be a hypocrite by continuing to complain about how ineffectively small businesses advertise without doing something to change it.

Trumped – Part 2 - You're hired!

"The greatest achievement of the human spirit is to live up to one's opportunities, and to make the most of one's resources."

— Luc De Vauvenargues

The last chapter of ADvice was titled "Trumped." It outlined a yearlong contest between two teams made up from my advertising department. Each team was assigned a business to work with over the next year. Each business was given up to $25,000 in advertising services from my company to use to their best advantage to grow their enterprise.

In true competitive style my staff picked the names for their teams: Perfect Marketing and Money Makers. The businesses they adopted were relatively new to our industry and definitely neophytes in terms of advertising. The goal for the teams was to use advertising to help these companies grow.

Upon the selection of the businesses, I was immediately blessed with an intense wave of gratitude from the business owners that truly touched me. I should have heeded the warning. One of the owners actually promised that she was writing to the editor of the Wall Street Journal to tell them of the extraordinary opportunity that my company was extending in this yearlong program. Everyone was happy. Everyone was excited. And I was confident that the lessons that were going to be learned would be profound and worthwhile.

My grandfather was a very folksy, yet dignified man. He sold memorial monuments (tombstones) for a living. He looked the part with white hair, an easy smile and a soft-spoken manner that belied his wisdom, which was won of years from dealing with people on both sides of the track. People loved and respected him. I think he knew I was destined to be in sales. Or maybe I am in sales because that was his legacy to me. Either way, his words and wisdom have always been my guide. One of his many lessons to me was, "The true value of anything is in direct proportion to the amount of your life you have to exchange in order to get it." Basically, he was telling me that anything I got for free was probably not of long-lasting value. And those things I really worked long and hard for would, in the end, become the most important things in my life. As I get older, his lessons come back to me, though too late sometimes. This occasion would be one of those times.

July of 2006 saw our two fledgling businesses and our two teams come together. Had it not been for the competition between the teams, my grandfather's words would be all that are needed in this column to explain the outcome of our contest. But salespeople are by nature competitive, and they love to win. In fact, our two teams each wanted to win so badly that they each counseled their assigned business far beyond typical advertising recommendations. What I had hoped would be a clearly black and white report on the merits of advertising turned into an intensive, complete, business-marketing plan. The advertising portion was planned out and scheduled early, while more strategic marketing ideas were played out over the remainder of the year. My intention to establish a baseline of performance, and then track performance improvements that had resulted solely from advertising's influence upon the businesses fell by the wayside as teams competed in ways that went beyond my original directive.

There is a principle that states that the mere act of observing something has an affect upon the outcome of the action being observed. If observation is redefined as focus, then the affect on the outcome is bound to be good. But if the observation is not focused, then confusion and inconsistency are bound to show up. I don't know where the whole thing got off track, but no baseline was established clearly enough to effectively track the nuances of different advertising influences on these businesses in spite of, or perhaps because of, the additional ideas and advice given to the owners. Sure, we have a great before and after picture, but unfortunately not enough specificity to say anything other than we know without a doubt that in both of these cases "advertising works."

Donald Trump might have "fired" some of our apprentices. But he would have also been impressed with the effort that both teams put forth. Our Perfect Marketing team generated a 505 percent annual sales increase for the business they consulted. While our second-place team, the Money Makers, only generated a 27 percent sales increase.

If I had gotten my wishes, I would have very definitive lessons that I could share from this experiment. But I didn't get the results I anticipated. The end results just did not fulfill my expectation. Then again, no good deed goes unpunished as we gained insights and expertise in areas where we were not looking. Our winning team combined media—print advertising with online banners and buttons. This success has contributed to our belief in Hybrid Marketing, which we are currently sharing with all of those advertisers who will listen.

In the end, the company came out ahead. The teams definitely learned how to help businesses with advertising, as well as in many other ways. Each of my salespeople and support staff contributed to a real-life success story, which is a great confidence builder. They not only know they can help a business grow with advertising and marketing suggestions, every one of them now has concrete proof they can do it. We have a much greater sense of teamwork among our staff. When a salesperson has a client problem, there are now several people he or she can immediately turn to for an expert opinion or solution.

At the risk of possibly offending our participating businesses, I am disappointed in the lack of follow-through and discipline displayed by both. My grandfather's words echo in my mind as I wonder why many of the opportunities offered to the businesses were squandered. I am certain that if I had asked them to put up $25,000 cash in an escrow account for one year, that would be returned after they complied with the terms of our agreement, each would have better communicated specific results that I could have shared with each of you. I didn't require a financial or an emotional investment by our businesses. And it's too bad, because they failed to realize as much from the experience as I know was available. Thank goodness I received a commitment from those on my staff to be on the winning team. It made the difference and also made them the bigger winners in the long run.

This year the MBA program at Taylor University in Upland, Ind., will be working with our sales staff and selected advertisers. Our goal is to provide more information with which our customers can make informed decisions about advertising. The more we know and the more of that knowledge we share, the better off we leave the world where we work and play. If you happen to be one of those advertisers we approach this year, please understand that just because we are not asking for thousands or tens of thousands of dollars, does not mean that we are not about to offer you great value in knowledge or greater value in potential growth for your company.

You cannot manage what you do not measure

"Making the simple complicated is commonplace; making the complicated simple, awesomely simple, that's creativity."

— Charles Mingus

Weekly sales numbers have reflected the grade card of my job performance for as long as I can remember. Week in and week out over the past 30 years, it has all come down to the numbers. Was I a nice guy? Did I do the right thing? Were the interests of my customers in the forefront of my mind? All of these things were secondary to the numbers. For the first few years in sales, I did everything I could do to avoid the weekly reality. I finally gave up and just surrendered to the results that the world used to judge my performance.

I gave in when I realized that my income was above many of my friends who did not have sales jobs. I worked commercial hours, basically 8 to 5 weekdays, when the majority of commercial businesses were open. My life was not bad by standards of personal income, work week and various other measures. That is when I came to grips with methodically managing myself. You see, I have this thing for wasted effort. My mother and my wife both choose to believe I am a little lazy. I, on the other hand, believe I have a healthy obsession for effectiveness, choosing only to put in effort that will yield a result—and preferably one that is positive. I don't like playing games that don't matter, and I never play games unless I intend to win. I have no use whatsoever for teammates that can be satisfied with moral victories. When it comes to work, I am much more serious. For I say, if it is worth doing, it is worth winning and annihilating your competition in the process.

Measuring my own performance began when I first started selling advertising. It seemed ad sales and I were made for each other. I did very well immediately. My first day, I earned more in commissions than I had made in the previous six months, proving to me I had a natural penchant for advertising. This early success, coupled with my desire to be the best, led me to develop measurements of my skills which I applied to every sales call I made. It didn't take more than six or eight weeks of feedback and adjustments before I was generating incredible sales results in terms of closing ratio and sales dollars. My confidence soared, and I literally felt I could outsell anyone.

For many years I consistently applied principles of measuring the effectiveness of my selling skills. When I got too confident from my results and got slipshod in measuring and managing my activities, my sales would slip, too. This not-so-kind reminder focused my need to revert to the one thing that led to my success: measuring the activities that led to my sales and minimizing those activities that did not lead to sales. It was about that time that someone gave me the slogan "you cannot manage what you do not measure." Since I had several years of outstanding growth in personal income, that slogan rang true.

As a manager, I learned how to differentiate personalities from performance. I developed a limited number of metrics that allows me to manage salespeople effectively. After many years of experience, I know I can rely upon them without question. My metrics have been tested by some of the best as well as some of the worst salespeople. The consistent results over the years from the metrics have led to the same conclusions and actions for adjusting sales performance.

For the last 24 years of managing salespeople and weekly sales figures, I can say I have prepared over 1,250 weekly sales reports. Week in and week out, I prepare these reports. Whether I am working in the office at my desk, traveling on business in a hotel room or on vacation with my family, Friday mornings find me assembling a sales report and determining what the numbers mean and how I can impact them the next week to achieve a higher level or increased quality. Ask me what Friday means to me, and I can assure you that no Friday is complete until I see the numbers, spend some time analyzing them and decide what, if anything can or needs to be done. You see, I also learned that management is the application of adjustments to the current state of activity. Too much adjustment can do damage, as well as too little adjustment. In many cases stability of direction is better than reacting to the bumps in the road we encounter everyday.

Leadership, management and driving a car all require that you stay on the road if you are to reach your goal in the most effective manner. The more you keep your attention in the distance, the smoother your course will be. Making adjustments by looking right in front of you will cause your trip to be erratic and take more time to complete. Leaders keep the vision of the destination in everyone's mind, and managers measure the daily progress toward the destination. Both acknowledge movement to create an awareness of progress and an environment of winning. The leader points to the accomplishment of the end result, and the manager celebrates the next step in the journey.

As an advertiser, you must lead and manage of the achievement of the goals of your business. As a leader, you must have the vision of where you wish to go, the ability to enroll those around you in getting there and be able to provide the inspiration for each of those involved in the journey. As the manager, you must measure each day's progress toward the goal, break down the contribution required from every employee, and maintain the resources necessary to keep everyone on course.

Far too often we let what we want influence us into forgetting the realities that rule us and divert our attention to doing it our own way. At times we become intoxicated with our own results and believe they are ours alone, when in reality they a borne of surrendering to measuring our progress and building on only those things that work. Performance is not us personally. Performance is the result of following what works and not following what does not work. The ability to get past ourselves and surrender to the equation of what works is not personal. Knowing the human condition, it is at times, heroic. But it is never personal.

Measuring sales metrics as I do each Friday is not extraordinary. Doing it every week for 1,250+ Fridays might be out of the ordinary. But you cannot manage what you do not measure. Find the metrics that move your business toward your goals. Record them each week. If they are low, find ways to increase them to the level you want. If they are just right or better than just right, find ways to sustain them by building structures that insure they can continue. Find your current state of activity through measurement and apply adjustments as necessary. Monitor the shifts in results you measure and continue to adjust accordingly as you continue your trip toward your predetermined success.

Don't be afraid of your negatives

"It doesn't matter what you want. What really matters is how much you want it. The extent and complexity of the problem does not matter as much as does the willingness to solve it."

— Ralph Marston

Every so often I tell my wife that I know I am not the most generous man in the world. She without hesitation agrees with my assessment. Given the right circumstances she even shares some more stringent and less complimentary opinions about my thrifty nature. But we agree that being thrifty is one of my less-favorable traits, from her perspective. My freely offered admission does buy me something. It gives me credibility in her eyes. When we do end up talking about finances, I fear she gives my knowledge and respect of money even more credit than I deserve.

It is a funny quirk of human nature that admission of a fault or shortcoming is gifted with an equal amount of belief and confidence in another area. A con man that leads with the comment that he is not very good with numbers can become sufficiently disarming enough to successfully separate his mark from his money. Mark Anthony in Shakespeare's play, Julius Caesar begins his soliloquy by damning the Caesar he ends up praising. The damning makes the praise even more powerful by contrast. These techniques of persuasion are very useful strategies for selling your products and positioning your business.

Researchers from Cleveland State University made a remarkable discovery in the mid-1980s when they sent identical candidates out to get job interviews with identical résumés and nearly identical letters of reference. The only difference was that one of the letters stated that the candidate could be "sometimes difficult to get along with." Of the two candidates the "difficult" candidate that got the most interviews. It seems that the admission of a fault made the glowing recommendations that much more credible.

Using this knowledge, one might want to think about developing an advertising campaign that begins with those things that you cannot do for a customer, and ends with just those unique services where you cannot be beat. I would be willing to bet that this honest approach to your limitations, coupled with your biggest selling point(s) would make a dynamite campaign. Why wouldn't you believe a company that is willing to bare its soul about those things it cannot do?

If I had to start my career in sales and advertising all over again, I'd develop a catchphrase for myself that would go something like this: "I can't fix your car nor can I help with your plumbing, but I am the one guy that can make your advertising work." I am fairly certain that if I had repeated that phrase rather than "I sell advertising," I would have been a much more memorable salesperson.

Normally at this point, I revert to my original theme and bring in another point. But I don't think it is good to dwell on the faults that my wife might or might not find in me, especially since she reads what I write, too. In my case, it is true that ignorance is bliss.

In my sales meetings I routinely ask my salespeople, "What are the two ways that people learn that are most applicable to advertising?" The answer is sequentially and through repetition. The first means that in order to understand something you must understand the basic concepts before you can be expected to understand the more advanced or complex concepts. This is why we teach our children the alphabet. Then we teach them how to spell and read three–five-letter words. They progress to reading and writing sentences and longer words. They continue with sequential steps until they can write paragraphs and finally term papers. You cannot expect a first grader to write a term paper and learn how to spell five-letter words at the same time. By natural sequence one precedes the other. Teaching people to learn sequentially about your products by means of your advertising is as critical to your business as our educational system is to the future of our country.

The other manner in which people learn is through repetition. Not one of us read through our ABCs one time and immediately knew them. Many of us still sing the song in our heads. Can you hear it? See how powerful an often-repeated sales message can be? Your sales message delivered with the same repetition of the ABC song would make all of us very rich. That degree of repetition is not easily achievable. But certainly, if it was your intention, you could find a level of repetition that outperforms all of your competitors in this area.

The trouble I have found with repetition is this: About the time you are just beginning to make progress with your customers and prospects, you are almost insane from hearing it so many times yourself. Then, if you can suspend your own sanity long enough to make an impact, you will still drop the campaign far too soon. This familiarity is the basis for the recent fiasco with the Aflac Duck. Even though the character had an 82-percent recognition factor by the public, the company's new chief marketing officer wanted to abandon it. Most likely it was because the repetition was driving Aflac people nuts. Cooler heads prevailed and an advertising icon continues. Maybe this form of insanity should be the new measuring stick for ad effectiveness.

There is a so much potential for repetition in advertising; it is too bad that advertisers become impatient and move on far too soon. I rarely see the same ad more than two, maybe three times in my magazines, when I know that a good ad could easily run 25 to 30 insertions before it begins to burn out audiences. I would rather see people spend ten times the amount on design and change ads/copy one-twelfth as often. They would save money, and would undoubtedly get the more-consistent results they actually desire.

Leading your presentation with a shortcoming should be matched with leaving your potential customers with a strong selling point. Studies show that no matter how much information is given to people, they most remember the first impression and the last impression. In the case of the first impression, I have no fear in mentioning my limitations. And in the case of the last impression, I can say with confidence that "I am the one guy that can make your advertising work." If that's all you get from this chapter, I have done my job.

Coaching

"Nothing will ever be attempted if all possible objections must be first overcome."

— Jules Lederer

"Have you ever noticed that in every field of human endeavor where performance counts, great coaching is integral to great performance -- except in business?" -- anonymous

During the recent Olympics many of us witnessed extraordinary individual and team performances. Each one that captivated and inspired us was made possible by exceptional coaching. The best athletes in the world submitted themselves to the oversight of coaches, who in most cases are not and never were as gifted or skilled on the field of competition. The athletes found great coaches so they could win. And they know that great coaches are committed as much, or more, to achieving victory as are most athletes.

World and Olympic records are important, as they measure the development of mankind in a physical sense. But the discipline of business affects the lives of so many more. There is an almost universal obsession to play the "Lone Ranger" in the business world. Businesspeople feel they must "do it themselves." Other than mentoring, a loose form of coaching, the bulk of businesspeople are left to perform without the benefit of coaching.

What would be possible if you and others in the business community not only accepted coaching, but embraced great coaching? What would you be capable of if someone held your performance to the standards you set for yourself? How good would you be if there was a coach who would not let you sell out on yourself when things get a little tough? How good could you be if someone pushed you at the very time you decided to rest, or when you felt you had given enough?

To get glimpse of what that might look like, you need to know what prevents effective coaching.

The first obstacle to effective coaching is when the performers believe they already know how to achieve the increased performance that both the coach and player are committed to. (Note: If they did know how, they would not have asked for or need the help of a coach). Coaching is almost exclusively action-results driven. Although many coaches may be knowledgeable, their knowledge is always in the background of their relationship with the performers and of whatever is the apparent moment of play or performance. In the foreground, the performer's actions generate results. Actions, not knowledge, create results.

Coaching is not about knowledge. Coaching is about results. Knowledge without results is pretty much useless. Knowledge allows you to believe you could create the result if you tried. However, in business, without results not many care what you know.

The next impediment to effective coaching is circumstances, reasons and excuses that are used to explain away undesired results. Circumstances, reasons and excuses are the panacea that makes mediocrity acceptable for the masses.

Too often performers believe that missing the desired result is okay, if you have a good enough reason. To the effective coach, circumstances, reasons and excuses are just part of the conditions the performer is responsible for, and the best result is not negotiable in light of these conditions. When performers accept responsibility for everything, progress comes quickly. Results need not be dependent upon circumstances, reasons or excuses. True performers generate great results in spite of them.

No effective coaching can occur if the performer focuses more on scoring points with the coach instead of producing a result on the field. Coaches take on performers that want to improve. Mistakes only happen when pushing limits. If the player is not pushing limits, he's playing on familiar ground and is more concerned with not making mistakes than with improving. Growth only exists on the other side of failure.

Effective coaching understands that failure fuels growth. Improvement comes through taking risks and making mistakes. Risk must be embraced, and failure never criticized; rather, it must be examined and overcome. For with failure comes growth and expertise, which is more valuable in the long term than the temporary set-back of a failed effort.

A final thing that prevents effective coaching is failure to surrender to coaching. Often coaches require a reorientation of actions that have become comfortable. Many times performers resist, wanting to remain with the usual or comfortable way they have done things in the past. This comes from what players know from personal experience, which may be limited; their fear of change is fear of the unknown. The coach's job is to empower the performer to play beyond his personal limits. This is only possible by surrendering to the coach's direction. Players must have blind trust in the coach's commitment to the result, and the performer must be able to push through being uncomfortable to get there.

Add to this list a universal need for individuals to "look good" in a business setting. The understanding that true growth occurs only through "failure" is not embraced in the business arena. Because of this many businesspeople limit themselves to attempt only what they "know" in order to avoid the ramifications and consequences of the cost of genuine growth.

Accepting coaching in the business world is seen as a weakness. Businesspeople universally want to be seen as strong and knowledgeable. The fiction we know as the "Lone Ranger," should be dressed in a business suit rather than wearing a mask and riding a white horse, for even in the Western version there is the trusty sidekick Tonto to make sure our Ranger is truly not alone.

Every four years I witness excellence in the summer Olympic Games – that excellence is result of extraordinary talent being guided by superb coaching in a variety of sports. I'm always awed by several performances, even though I expect to see the best. Unfortunately, during the intervening time, I cannot remember witnessing any businesses whose performances inspired me in any similar fashion.

My advice is to commit to setting your own world record with your business. Find a coach who will totally commit to the highest standard of results, and who will ruthlessly hold you to achieving the goals you set for yourself and your business. When all is said and done, you will be happy, no matter where you end up. For, I can promise that your talent, plus great coaching, will enable you to achieve more than you could ever achieve by yourself.

The Dominator

"People are always blaming their circumstances for what they are. I don't believe in circumstances. The people who get on in this world are the people who get up and look for the circumstances they want, and, if they can't find them, make them."

— George Bernard Shaw

In 1984, Arnold Schwarzenegger became the world's most famous cyborg in the film "The Terminator." Until then none of us imagined that a man-made robot would have an accent. Today most of us cannot imagine a 21st century cyborg that doesn't speak as if it is from Eastern Europe. The character played by Schwarzenegger was the personification of a relentless single-minded obsession. Its sole purpose was to kill the movie's heroine, Sarah Connor. As the movie unfolds, the audience is left to discover that the terminator was sent back in time from a future world to change events so the future would be different. In 1984, the pace, the chase and the intensity of the movie was breathtaking, as nothing could stop the Terminator's relentless pursuit of the heroine.

This is a great model for the novice advertiser. Just as the cyborg in the movie relentlessly tracks the hero and heroine, you must be similarly obsessed with reaching your customer. Your media plan should target your customer, and with the same fanatical obsession stay in front of them until they buy or they die.

How do you do this? You dominate the media that you buy. To dominate, you should buy bigger and/or more ads than your competitor in every issue of the magazine. Buy special packages that offer you value-added exposure in special listings such as website listings, geographical listings or organizational membership listings. Buy multiple placements: spreads, inserts, gatefolds, etc. Become The Dominator by dominating every place you advertise. You will get better rates and, most importantly, you will get better results.

Far too many advertisers believe that if you tell ten million people about yourself one time, you will generate enough interest to do a bunch of business. Reality and experience show, however, that telling one hundred thousand people about yourself one hundred times (still 10 million impressions), is a far more effective strategy. And you can do this by using more frequency in fewer places. This gives you the added advantage of quantity discounts through buying more frequency. You dominate every place that your message is available. So your impact goes up as your overall advertising costs go down. You also end up dealing with fewer different media which adds to your personal effectiveness.

The Dominator uses additional strategies, like buying a couple one-third vertical ads in addition to a full page ad. The one-third verticals dominate the pages where they are placed because publishers build ad pages from the outside lower corners of the page and work inward and upward. A one-third vertical is the first ad to be placed on a page with multiple ads. And it is also the size and layout that most often gets a page of its own. This size and layout is almost as effective as a full-page and certainly more cost efficient than a one-half page ad. The full-page plus a couple one-third verticals give the appearance of dominating a publication.

Buying simple programs like web listings and geographical listings are positions that usually run in every issue. The costs are usually very reasonable and for a few dollars offer one more exposure within the same issue.

Gatefolds are the pages of a magazine that fold out to create a larger page. We all get the vision of the "centerfold" when we think of this vehicle. The fact is that gatefolds guarantee exposure because the pages of the magazine naturally break open to a gatefold insert because it is where the heaviest paper is placed in the magazine.

Center-spreads are left-right full page ads that take two full pages in the layout. These seem more important because they take up the reader's entire field of vision when they turn to these pages. Do the results double? Not statistically, but they do send the message to the customer, the prospect, and even those not interested that the advertiser is in fact The Dominator.

Dominators purchase fixed positions. The inside front cover, inside back cover and outside back cover positions, pages 3, 5, 7 and the page across from the inside back cover are premium locations generally held by the advertising leaders in the industry. Other print vehicles include faux covers or cover wraps where an advertiser's four-page ad actually wraps over the magazine's cover. Belly bands are those paper bands that wrap around magazines and many publications offer these as advertising vehicles. All types of inserts, such as calendars and posters, are great for exposure as advertisers give away something of perceived value that will be useful for a longer period of time.

Building your image is not a sometime thing. You must do it every day and become consistent. The only way to be dominant is to play big where you play, and not playing unless you can play big. The benefit is obvious: you get the lion's share of the business available, rather than fighting with other little guys over the crumbs left by the current Dominator. It does not take a lot of money to become the top dog, only discipline to stick with the plan, especially when it is working. When you begin to feel that you are the winner, do not cut back (as many believe they can). At this point, you can clearly become The Dominator by denying any competitor the ability to get a foothold in your market.

Will you became The Dominator immediately? No. You will only become dominant as you buy more and bigger ads. The process is cumulative, building as time goes on. Unfortunately, it also dies the same way. As you lighten up and others take your position, it is not a black and white change. It is much more gradual and insidious than that. By the time you are no longer The Dominator and it will take more than saying "I'll be back" for you to return."

How much is enough?

"If one advances confidently in the direction of his dreams, and endeavors to live the life which he has imagined, he will meet with a success unexpected in common hours."

— Henry David Thoreau

My career in advertising has been blessed. I have met many of the legends of the advertising industry as well as notables in the entertainment industry. I have been around long enough that there are few situations I have not encountered. After dealing with thousands of small businesses, it is easy to believe that nine out of ten new businesses fail. I know because over half of my clients over my business lifetime no longer exist. I'm proud to say that the ones I worked with lasted longer than the ones who chose not to work with me.

Am I that good? I really wish it were true. But the hard fact is this: Advertising works, and those who do not believe in advertising, engage in advertising, and plan for advertising are doomed to have their businesses fail faster than others. Since the first knight put his family crest on the shield he used in battle, advertising has announced the arrival of new products and services. Advertising is really that good.

Early in my career I worked with quite a few advertisers who asked me how much was enough to spend on advertising. Many years later, I recognize that the number who asked that question in those formative years of my career was disproportionate to the percentage of prospects who would normally ask that question. Still, it gave me a very unique perspective as I began my career. How much is enough?

Oddly enough, I would like to point out that at this time, every single one of the advertisers who asked that question, all of them are still in business today. Some have gone through radical changes. Others are remarkably similar to the business I called on many years ago. But ten out of ten of them are still around in one form or another.

The answer to the question is very simple. To find the answer, do not look at the question, look at the results. It is like breathing air. How much is enough? Believe me: when it is not enough, you will know. You breathe whatever air it takes. The same should be true for your advertising. Spend whatever it takes to do the job.

Think about it. What if you spent just one dollar too little? Every other dollar that you spend is, in essence, wasted. Too many people do this. They create some arbitrary formula and decide that it is a rule not to be broken. Many businesspeople spend almost to the level of success. When they do not spend enough they look at advertising like it is the culprit, failing to understand what it takes to achieve the goal. If advertising were a science instead of an art, some mathematician would develop a formula that would work every time. Saying it is an art is only because we acknowledge that there are far too many measurable factors that affect advertising that cannot be controlled. However, the human mind is intuitive enough to give most astute marketers a "feel" for what will work and what will not work.

Most folks want cut and dried answers. Is the correct budget 5.375% of last year's gross sales or net sales? Do I need to spend 1.5 times that amount to achieve growth? What if I spend too much? Believe me, never have I found a businessperson who spends too much on advertising. I have seen many spending unwisely, but I cannot remember anyone spending too much. People want a formula for figuring budgets so they can blame the results on the formula and take themselves off of the hook. But businesspeople are always on the hook for their results. Once you accept that responsibility, you are more likely to spend adequately to achieve your goal. At 100% responsibility, it is much easier to decide how much is enough.

It is budget time and I hate budgets. For me, expense budgets are constraints, not the guidelines they are intended to be. Like nearly everyone else, I procrastinate on getting my completed budget submitted. I am good at achieving my sales goals but not because I follow my budget. I manage my sales on a results basis. I spend to achieve results, and often spend until I achieve results. You see, I discovered many years ago, that revenue targets that are achieved or surpassed make up for a multitude of budget sins. Conversely, a balanced budget that fails to reach its sales goal is really worth nothing.

As you do your budget this year, ask yourself, "Am I spending enough?" You can always cut back if you lose your confidence. But in asking the question, you just might find the answer to finally making your advertising budget pay off.

Buzz – the ultimate goal of advertising

"The best ad is a good product."

— Alan H. Meyer

My colleagues cringe when I agree with many other business people that word-of-mouth advertising is the best form of advertising. My colleagues believe that I am agreeing with a strategy of avoiding paid media advertising in favor of word of mouth. You see, a belief in word-of-mouth advertising is one of the most common objections to purchasing paid media we receive when speaking to potential advertisers. Many potential advertisers fear being sold something they don't want, and that fear causes many of them to tell advertising salespeople that they only rely on word-of-mouth advertising.

The irony of that statement comes to light when many of them say this while exhibiting at a trade show, a very expensive form of advertising where the advertiser transports his product, himself and other portions of his business to a centralized location where a select number of buyers gather to purchase product. In the 1980s, trade shows were one of the most expensive ways to market products. With today's rising costs of travel, unionized labor on the show floors, products costs, etc., trade shows are not becoming any better bargains today.

Trade shows are the least cost-effective way to advertise products. Even the smallest exhibitor is going to spend at least $3,000 for an industry-event trade show. Considering that most exhibitors speak with no more than 150 potential customers at the show that equates to a $20,000 CPM (cost per thousand). Advertising rates for trade (business-to-business) magazines, industry trade journals, etc., run from $35 to $100 CPM. Why would anyone attend these shows with such high costs? The answer: buzz.

Word-of-mouth advertising occurs when one consumer tries a product and is impressed enough to share his positive experience with others. The more positive the experience, the less risk involved, and the more trusted the source of the endorsement, the better the results in word-of-mouth advertising in terms of generating more sales. Word of mouth is so effective, that for many years, advertisers have employed recognizable people and have paid them to endorse products. Advertisers have played upon the trust built by certain personalities to sell their products. All because they know that word-of-mouth advertising is so much more effective than any other form. When an advertiser cannot find our close personal friends, they hire a substitute personality, usually a celebrity that is easily recognizable and scores high in credibility with target audiences. It is not as good as hearing it from a friend or trusted advisor, but still, a spokesperson is one of the most effective advertising strategies.

True buzz comes from consumers, purveyors and industry experts who are impressed with a product and recommend that product to friends and others. Companies who attend trade shows hope that the few customers they encounter will leverage the large trade-show expense by buying their products and recommending those products to their colleagues. Too few companies understand the value of finding these passionate consumers. If they did, they would use mass-advertising techniques to locate advocates that exist for their products lines. These advocates account for a large volume of sales by recommending the products to friends, colleagues and total strangers, if the endorser's job is to make recommendations. Most businesses attending trade shows find heavy users or influencers, and treat them as a single consumer. This expectation limits the experience for the customer and highly motivated person who might have become an advocate, but becomes simply a customer. And there are very few companies that can afford to spend the $3,000+ on the low number of potential customers available at a trade show.

The Anatomy of Buzz: How to Create Word-of-Mouth Marketing by Emanuel Rosen, a Currency book published by Doubleday, outlines the importance of word-of-mouth advertising. The mere recommendation of any product from a trusted source can often lead to outstanding success of a new product introduction. Editors from magazines in my company are bombarded with requests to review and endorse products. Any company wishing such review should first read and understand Mr. Rosen's book, for a product review is little good if you do not know what to do with it.

Like all other advertising, word of mouth will accelerate the failure of a poor product as quickly as it can lead to the success of an excellent product. Unfortunately, word of mouth is largely ineffective with the promotion of mediocre products, since many of them are not worthy of conversation. This is something that those folks I mentioned at the beginning of this column do not understand. Only very good products or very poor products respond well to word-of-mouth advertising. The more of a staple that the product is, the less opportunity exists for it to qualify for word-of-mouth endorsement. Can you imagine being at a gathering, say a picnic, and actively talking about a new brand of straight pin? Hardly. Even if you were talking to another sewing enthusiast, you are more likely to talk about the weather. However, if you were sufficiently impressed with a new fabric-cutting product, you might share that experience. After you did, someone else might approach, the subject might change or the conversation take a different direction. The point is that your mention is going to be balanced by your experience, and the importance of that product in your overall experiences. Advertisers want this conversation, but too few realize that mass advertising is the common denominator that can stimulate such an exchange.

A couple of years ago the success of the book A Purpose-Driven Life and the movie The Passion of Christ were both driven by word-of-mouth advertising. Key consumers were located in both instances and were targeted for advertising messages. These consumers became advocates and were targeted for even more promotional efforts. As more and more effort was focused at this group, the more the group recommended the products to relatives, friends and eventually total strangers. In the case of the book, the passionate core bought several copies to give as gifts. In the case of the movie, the core advocates took friends and relatives to the movie.

If you are going to utilize word-of-mouth advertising, first begin with an exceptional product. A mediocre product will take too much effort, and a poor product will fail far too quickly. Next, make sure that the consumers you select to be your advocates have an extraordinary experience with your product. Take the time to make sure they have a "WOW" experience. The more memorable it is, the more it will be shared with others. Make sure you look at these few users as an investment. If possible, supply your advocates with a few product samples to share in the case of consumables, or discount coupons in the case of long-life products, so they have a head-start on becoming an evangelist for your brand. Keep your advocates on the inside. Inform them about new developments, awards, price breaks, sales, etc. In essence, continue to give them positive things to share about your product. Use mass advertising to continue to build this core of loyal consumers. Yes, pay to advertise. But understand your purpose is to build this core. Continue to grow your core to a critical mass. Build fanatical customer loyalty by returning loyalty to your customers in the form of product improvements, price reductions, or anything else you can do to increase the quality equation of your offering.

Like the evangelist in a traveling tent revival, find the followers of your product in each city and share with them the gospel of your products. Ask them to spread the word about your company and products as you continually reaffirm their importance by acknowledging them.

The Anatomy of Buzz suggests that advertising is the best way to stimulate buzz. Media advertising jump-starts the process and can accelerate product sales quickly. Advertising is not very effective in simulating buzz. Even endorsements by a credible company spokesperson, do not come close to the credibility of a recommendation of a non-paid source known to the consumer. And yes, advertising can kill buzz. If consumers feel that advertisers are trying pulling a fast one by attempting to stimulate buzz, they will revolt by distrusting the product.

Using pre-existing social connections to increase awareness of your product, known as "viral marketing," can be very effective. Yet almost every expert will tell you that viral marketing works as well or better with a branded (advertised) product than with an unknown, suggesting that viral marketing is not a substitute for advertising, but quite possibly an extension.

So the next time you are tempted to tell someone that you rely only on word-of-mouth advertising, beware—it may be me. If it is, I will engage you in a discussion about what consumers you are targeting as the most likely group to carry your word-of-mouth message. I will ask you to point out the product features so remarkable that they cause consumers to endorse your product to their friends. And finally, I'll recommend to you that media advertising is the most effective manner to expand and stimulate further word-of-mouth advertising, thus expanding additional product sales.

Competition

"Heroes are ordinary men and women who dare to see and meet the call of possibility – Bigger than themselves. Breakthroughs are created by heroes, by men and women who will stand for the result while it is only a possibility, people willing to create a path to the result, while others are still squabbling about the "right path" and arguing about the "right answers" – people who will act now, to make possibility real today.

— Werner Erhard

Much is made today of our professional athletes. They are bigger than life, and you see them everywhere. It almost seems like you must be a celebrity before you can become a Hall of Fame athlete, rather than the other way around.

The whole phenomenon is interesting when viewed through the eyes of advertising. The art of advertising has become so advanced in sports that many amateurs become famous before they have played their first professional match. Sports agents can take the credit for this. Their fees are based upon a percentage of the contracts they negotiate for the athletes they represent. The bigger the claims made about their client, the larger will be the resulting contract, and hence, the bigger the agent's fee.

It is interesting how agents spin the statistics of their clients in order to show them in the best light. It used to be if the athlete's team won a lot of games, they undoubtedly were good at the position they played. Today, quarterbacks are measured on dozens of statistics including third conversions on the final drive of the games they've played. Or how many different receivers they have thrown to and completed passes, as if the receiver's ability to catch passes is totally the quarterback's responsibility.

There are multitudes of measurements in every sport designed to quantify an athlete's talents, skills and predictable behavior. All of them are designed to figure out one thing—can he (she) win? In spite of these statistics and measurements, more athletes fail to make the professional level than the number of those who succeed. Of those who become successful in the professional ranks, many are unknowns. They are unknown in terms of not having an outstanding amateur career. Why is that? How can someone who is not acknowledged as the best of the best become a solid professional athlete?

I believe it is the one thing nobody has found a way to measure: competitive spirit. There are some athletes, like Lance Armstrong, the cyclist, Doug Flutie, the diminutive quarterback, and other seemingly ordinary people who have been defined as winners, solely because of this trait. Their natural talent is not extraordinary. In some cases their skills and demonstrative talents are not even close to many of their colleagues. Yet they win because they refuse to be beaten. These people love to compete.

Often this intangible quality is called "heart," a romantic term which attempts to define a single person's determination to win. This characteristic has become romanticized to the point that it is the most desirable trait sought in professional athletes. It is based on a love of competition and on the ability and desire to use all of the skills and talents at one's disposal to win the game he or she is engaged in playing.

We all need to compete. We need to compete in our businesses. We need to compete in our jobs. Competition defines the result of our efforts. Without strong competition, we fail to give our all. It cheats us out of giving our best, and it cheats our customers by providing them with a little less than the best product or service.

In our capitalist society, competition drives our economy. Without competition, there is no urge to improve. This is no urgency to even win. Without competition, apathy toward our product or service leads to dissatisfied customers and a less vigorous marketplace.

There are few things more gratifying than becoming successful in an area where aggressive competition exists. Competition validates your effort. It gives you a benchmark to measure your own talent and skill. When all other rewards fail, competition fulfills us.

If you are like me, you have a relative in your family that you look up to. As a younger man, it was my uncle. I idolized him, and I always wanted to please him. I asked him to play games with me. Those times when he challenged me and beat me, I worked hard, was out of breath and was taxed by my effort, but I knew I gave it my all. I felt good and measured my advancement by the severity of the beating I took.

But there were also times when my uncle tried to be kind to me by letting me win. He lowered the level of competition. Even though I won, I was not satisfied. Neither of us enjoyed it, and winning did nothing to help me improve my skills or hone my talents, much less my confidence.

This uncle is no longer with us, and I miss being challenged by him. As I grew older, he would challenge me intellectually. He defeated me as long as he could. We eventually became equals, and I often was able to defeat him in many areas. But our relationship, by and large, was based in getting the best out of the other, and we enjoyed every minute of it.

School children today are not being challenged the way I was. Political correctness has made everyone afraid to stimulate competition. Instead, teachers are finding ways to avoid measurements of comparison, so they don't hurt children's feelings. That's too bad. We are training a generation to become dull and unengaged. They are failing to learn the lessons of competition. But an even more terrible loss is that these children do not understand that disappointment and elation are on the same continuum. Without experiencing one, you can fully appreciate the other.

Dolly Parton once said, "If you want to enjoy the rainbow, you must tolerate the rain." In avoiding competition, we are raising a group of children who may be doomed to only experience the middle of their emotional range. We are training them to avoid attempting to become a winner because of a fear of losing. We may very well be deprogramming the next Lance Armstrong, erasing in our children the intangible "heart" that we all admire so much in our sports heroes and heroines.

Competition in our businesses is important. It is an integral ingredient in our capitalist model. It drives us to perform. It stimulates advancement and innovation. Competition creates in each of us a confidence and willingness to pick ourselves up and start all over. The feeling of winning is so addictive that, like a mother who is willing to go through the pain of childbirth for the experience having another baby, we are willing lose many times over in our attempt to feel that exhilaration of winning.

There are not enough of us in the business world who are acknowledged for having "heart." Many of us win only because we desire to win, not because we are the best-prepared or the best-educated. We just really detest losing.

The next time your competitor beats you. Don't get mad, get to work. Thank your competitor for driving innovation in your business category. Thanks to your competitor, you are as good as you are today. Thanks to your competitor, tomorrow you will be better. And thanks to your competitor, you can get genuine satisfaction and enjoyment from what you do.

"Friends, Romans, Countrymen..."

"Next to Christianity, advertising is the greatest force in the world. And I say that without sacrilege or disrespect. Advertising makes people discontented. It makes them want things they don't have. Without discontent, there is no progress, no achievement."

— Ray Locke

Persuasion is an art form that too few businesspeople take the time to study. Mark Anthony's speech to the citizens of Rome in William Shakespeare's Julius Caesar is one of the very best examples of persuasion I could point out. Act 3, Scene 2 of Shakespeare's classic play finds conspirator Brutus placating a crowd of Roman citizens, and leaving Mark Antony, a Roman general and close friend of Caesar, to speak to the crowd over the assassinated leader's body.

The speech is too long to replicate in this column, but when it is read in context, it is a perfect example of the art of persuasion, using many speaking techniques that impart power to the message being given. Antony disarms his audience in the opening phrases of the speech: "Friends, Romans, countrymen, lend me your ears; I come to bury Caesar, not to praise him." He positions the assassins against Caesar: "The evil that men do lives after them; the good is oft interred with their bones; so let it be with Caesar. The noble Brutus hath told you Caesar was ambitious: If it were so, it was a grievous fault, and grievously hath Caesar answer'd it." In succeeding passages he continues to undercut the credibility of Brutus and the rest who participated in the murder of Caesar.

Later, Antony says that he loved his friend Caesar, and even though the conspirators would tell his countrymen that they should not love Caesar, they would remember that they loved him, too, when they learned how much Caesar loved them by remembering them in his will. Then Antony takes it away from the crowd by saying that he should not tell them that in Caesar's will, the people are his heirs, for "it will inflame you." He just poured fuel on the flames.

In a final passage of persuasion, Antony reads Caesar's will and tells the crowd how Caesar remembered each of them individually and collectively because he loved them so much. By then the crowd was an angry mob, ready for revenge against Brutus and Cassius who led the assassination of the leader.

People can be persuaded if they think you can reward them, or if they think you can punish them. An impending incentive or threat adds weight to words intended to persuade. Antony's mention of Caesar's will offered the hope of reward, thus swaying the crowd to the point of view that Caesar was not a cruel dictator, but a beneficent one. A little more veiled was the threat against those who would side with Brutus and Cassius. With seeming sincerity, Antony first states that the conspirators are "honorable men." As he contrasts their actions against poor Caesar, who loved his citizens, he speaks the words with more and more sarcasm, which changes the implication of his words from good men to indicate that the assassins are dishonorable men.

People can be persuaded if you have bonded with them. Antony bonded with the crowd by separating himself initially from Caesar, and from Brutus and Cassius as well. He bonded with the crowd by sharing his feelings and by pointing out Caesar's generosity to them all. He created distance from the conspirators by showing the crowd Caesar's blood-stained robe, and by describing the blows Caesar sustained from the daggers of those "honorable" men.

People can be persuaded if they think you have more expertise than they do. By stating that he knew Caesar, Antony in essence told the crowd that he was in a position to judge the dictator because he knew Caesar's heart.

People can be persuaded if the situation limits their options. Antony gave the crowd the illusion of options, but created a situation that limited how they could react when he mentioned Caesar's will. How could you hate a dictator who loved you so much that he remembered you in his will?

Even if you have no desire to read Shakespeare's Julius Caesar, studying Act 3, Scene 2 of the play is one of the best lessons in persuasion that you could take. Although the interplay with the crowd is predictable and not orchestrated as well as the speech, Antony's words are crafted as well as any persuasive speech you will ever read.

Persuasion is like building a maze that ultimately leads to the result you desire, and then allowing the rats to run to their hearts' content. You know all along that they will show up at the end of the maze, exactly where you planned.

That's great for an orator, or even a salesperson, but what about a businessperson who advertises? The secrets of persuasion can make good advertising copy great. The difference between mediocre results and a home run often lies more in the finesse of persuasion than the in the advertising strategy itself.

Studying persuasion, even if only for a few hours, could be one of the best investments you ever make into advertising effectiveness. A single word in the context of an entire paragraph can be the difference between black and white. Knowing which authorities audiences will identify with, and be persuaded, or dissuaded by, is useful in the crafting of advertising copy. But even more, understanding what strings are being pulled will allow you to become less a puppet tomorrow than you may be today.

Too few of our contemporaries understand the great art of persuasion. Today persuasion is a talent too often forsaken for hyperbole at best and outright falsehoods at worst. Well-crafted understatement is in short supply. I tire of sorting through exaggerated claims that are hard to believe no matter how optimistic your point of view might be.

Persuasion uses logical arguments and language to sway others to a new point of view. In Shakespeare's play, Mark Antony's reasoning and rhetoric craft a new image of the assassinated dictator Julius Caesar as the beloved benefactor of Rome. "Here was a Caesar! When comes such another?"

The $15 Cadillac

Product pricing is a marketing art that few have mastered. The better companies continually test pricing levels of their products. Very few use pricing to establish positioning of their products and/or their companies. Too many businesses typically decide to price their products and/or services based upon how they perceive themselves when compared to their competitors. Obviously, there must be some connection with reality when it comes to pricing—isn't there? After many years in this business, I would say the answer is much closer to no, than it is to yes.

Many years ago while running a radio station; I became friends with Rita Runyon, who at that time ran a market-research company in South Bend, Ind. Her company did a few listener-research projects and focus groups for my radio station. Rita invited me to take part in a taste test she was conducting for a major brewery. I thought the experience would be fun and was convinced that being an ad guy, I would not be confused by all of the slick marketing applied by this industry. The end result was that I could not tell the difference between a popular premium beer and a popular light beer. I opted for the premium beer, which I did not drink at the time, and gave a thumbs-down to the brand I had been drinking for a few years. That experience convinced me to my core that perception is reality. And to be effective, you must only control perception.

You see, I used to believe, with all things being equal; the percentage of product margin is inversely proportional to the maturity of the product category. New products have high margins to recapture the huge research expense invested in the development of the product. As the innovation becomes more commonplace, competitive pressures require prices to fall in order to maintain market share of the aggressive market growth of new consumer purchases. As the market approaches saturation, product pricing further falls, even with product enhancements that surpass the original innovation. Only when the market is saturated and sales become more or less replacement purchases, will wild fluctuations in pricing subside.

After my beer-tasting experience I began to notice how nearly everyone responded more congruently with their perception of a product than to the realities of the marketplace. The answers you receive when you ask people how much margin (profit) there is in the price of some items always intrigues me. In many cases, consumers believe no matter what the price of a product, the profit margin is nearly the same for products in the same category. For example, they believe that a discount beer selling for $2.49 per six-pack has the same margin as a premium beer selling for $6.29 per six-pack. Consumers believe the difference is in the quality of the product. Granted, the $6.49 beer may be a better product, but the ingredients are not two and three-quarters times more expensive. Actually, the biggest difference is in the perception of the quality of the product.

In the early 1990s, I owned and operated a company that sold merchandising programs to retail grocers. During that period, I had the opportunity to work with a lot of companies that manufactured and processed food products. I was surprised to discover that the same processing plants that canned vegetables for major brand names also canned the same vegetables for chain-store private labels. In some cases the products were all canned at the same time with the line stopping only to change the labels that went on the cans. At retail, the brand-name items sold for a higher price point than the store-brand or private-label product, even though everything was exactly was the same. The investment into the "brand image" gave the consumer more confidence, and that translated into consumers feeling better about paying higher prices for the brand-name product.

There is a range beyond which buyers will not allow themselves to be fooled. We all desire to make prudent purchases. Our "value" meter is balanced with the actual price versus what we perceive as quality. There are times when we find ourselves without adequate information, so we make a judgment about a product's quality as if its value is based solely upon price. "Brain surgery $2,500 or $75,000—which would you choose?" "Used Cadillac: $15 will buy it today." Do you see how you make judgments about things you don't fully understand, based upon the information you think you have?

Understanding how people judge pricing, you may want to consider very carefully how to position your products, and hence your entire company, among competitors. I suggest that being in the middle of the pack is the worst place to be. Once you price yourself as better than some and not as good as others, the consumer is going to view you as "adequate." And as long as you can have special pricing from time to time, consumers will buy adequate at an inexpensive price for a bargain. "Adequate" as a position is not the first place where consumers go.

Far worse is to take commodity pricing (lowest price) if you intend to have a business cycle that is other than what commodity sales will give you, that rise and fall with market trends. When you choose the lowest price, the consumer suspects that quality is going to be average to mediocre. There are some very good areas to take advantage of this strategy. If you are currently alone in a market, this strategy can insure that other competitors have a very hard time entering the market. Production ramp-up costs make it prohibitive to start a business to compete in commodity markets without other strong advantages. It still does not make you bulletproof. Take, for instance, the case of toilet tissue. Many years ago, before Charmin, there was no product differentiation for this product, and hence, toilet tissue was viewed as a commodity market controlled by price alone. Charmin claimed a position of better quality, as well as an improved customer experience and established a strong market share they still defend today.

There are other benefits of taking the premium-priced position. The biggest advantage is that you can actually make a better product than most of your competitors. The incremental costs in manufacturing a superior product rarely run more than an additional 15–20 percent in product. This premium-priced position can realize as much as 25 percent more in retail pricing. The increase in margin, then, is much more than just increase in cost. An example is a widget costing $1 to produce; it sells at retail for $3.95 with a gross margin of $2.95. By using better materials, that same item might cost $1.15 to manufacture, but could sell at retail for a higher price of $4.95, giving a margin of $3.80. Some margins, depending upon the product line, could approach doubling the amount of profit, giving the company the ability to establish a strong brand image, as well as take more profit to the bottom line.

If you remember that perception is far more important than reality in pricing, you can choose the perception you want to build around your product with not only your advertising, but also your pricing. As a matter of fact, make sure that perceptions of your product and your pricing are congruent, or you, too, could be selling a $15 Cadillac.

Leadership

"You can say the right thing about a product and nobody will listen. You've got to say it in such a way that people will feel it in their gut. Because if they don't feel it, nothing will happen."

— William Bernbach

Being the boss, being in charge and even being responsible, does not make anyone a leader. It just means you hold a title, you have the authority to make the decisions, and the buck stops at your desk. We have many people in management positions today that are often mistaken for leaders. Leadership is not about any of that.

I had writer's block about what to write for this last column of 2007. When this happens, I look through my bookshelf for inspiration. Today I picked up a book titled Heroz, Empower Yourself, Your Coworkers, Your Company by William C. Byham and Jeff Cox. This book is the second of a duo on employee empowerment. Zapp! The Lightning of Empowerment by the same authors was a cornerstone in the development of my current management philosophy.

In my mind's eye I equate most companies to a Roman galley, in terms of structure, where the captain up on top of the deck at the stern by the ship's rudder. The managers are like the hands that are running around on the upper deck, and the line employees are below deck shackled to long oars extending out the sides of the ship that they attempt to pull in unison to move the ship in the desired direction. More often than not the captain is so busy watching where the ship is going that he does not have contact with the line employees. The managers each want to look good for the captain, so they run about the upper deck attempting to appear as if they are busy, which gives the captain confidence in his chosen direction. These managers are too busy on the upper deck to attend to the below-deck needs. And finally, those line employees responsible for the physical work of getting the ship to its destination are chained below deck having no idea if the ship is on course or not.

Leadership by definition requires followers not subordinates. Being a follower is pretty much a voluntary role. Although many can be placed in the subservient position of physically following, only in the presence of leadership can someone be inspired to become a follower. In the scenario above there is no leader. The captain is definitely the boss with ruthless absolute authority. He is also without question in charge. And he may very well have sole responsibility for reaching his destination. But nobody is following. It is easy to assume the mangers are being coerced, most likely motivated by fear of not doing what is required of them. And definitely the line employees are being pushed by a supervisor to achieve their goal. Many times on Roman ships the pushing involved whips and clubs.

The reason I like the two books mentioned above is that they are written from the perspective that employees all come to work and want to do a good job. I've always believed that to be true. It is not human nature to go after a job with the initial goal of trying to cheat your company. That type of motivation, if it does occur, does not materialize until many false starts and frustrating missteps put the employee's goals and those of the company at odds. All in all, people take a job not just to make money, but more importantly, they want to make a difference.

If you ask any people what they want out of life and drill down to their most basic instincts by questioning their responses with the query "why?," you will eventually get to "I want to make a difference." The human condition cries out such that we want our very existence to be meaningful by purposely affecting the lives of others and being recognized for doing so. In the end, we all want leave our mark on the world with the desire to have it recognized while we are still here. This is probably the single most compelling motivation known to human beings, beyond the survival instinct. This desire to be known and acknowledged is primal. It can be a leader's most effective tool.

Leadership inspires with a vision for building something. Management motivates by avoidance of consequences. Leaders pull others forward by example. Managers coerce compliance with rules and structure. Leadership empowers. Management guides. Managers say what's happening now. Leaders say what's happening next.

Leaders know that every individual wants to be honestly acknowledged for making a difference. Great leaders provide individuals the opportunity to make a difference within the framework of the leader's vision, and then they acknowledge them for doing so. Great managers get the job done and move on to the next agenda item.

I've had the honor to follow great leadership. It is a wonderful experience. Leaders call people to be better than they see themselves. A great leader makes you feel better about yourself, and inspires you to improve. They draw you into a vision of the future by empowering you to make a difference. Leaders create a beneficial environment by acknowledging achievement. Great leaders have great visions that include the contributions of everyone. And they have the ability to communicate how each individual is part of and necessary to the complete fulfillment of their vision. Great leaders pull extraordinary performance from individuals. Individuals strive to perform for those whom they respect.

Great leaders are always in pursuit of their visions and yell over their shoulders for others to come join them in the quest. Some leaders are the boss and some are not. Some are in charge and some are not. Some are responsible and some are not. Leadership knows no position. It only knows leadership. Being a leader requires nothing more than the existential act of courage of stepping up to lead as the need appears.

Most importantly leaders assume others want to make a difference. Leaders work harder at providing employees openings to fulfill that need, than they do finding employees being dishonest or lazy. Expectations have a funny way of being fulfilled. If the expectation is to find someone trying to cheat the company, then perception, intuition and the actions manifest from them will certainly make it come true at some point. But if the expectation is to find passion and commitment to the vision from employees, then passionate employees is the result that will eventually occur.

The books by Byham and Cox assume that all employees want to be champions, and the only thing holding them back from being so is their boss, their arbitrary company rules and an almost universal ignorance of the human need for acknowledgement. It would be a remarkable company that could take on total empowerment as described in these books. Managers would stop managing things and begin leading and coaching employees. Individuals would contribute their best efforts and acknowledge their own performance based upon honest criteria they set for themselves. And everyone would seek approval from the only place it really matters, the customer.

Doesn't this sound like a wonderful dream for a new year? Yes. But that probably won't happen. It is so much easier to manage numbers rather than to lead people. Managing numbers dehumanizes individual performance and nearly takes the human element completely out of the equation. Then in business, those pesky customers are the only ones left to deal with. Customers are tolerated because of their cash. If only there were a way ...

Some men have dreams that are only good ideas. Leaders communicate these dreams as visions perceived as fulfillable by all whom they inspire to follow.

Rocket Science

"To think that the effects of advertising, such a potent environment in any industrialized country, could be limited to economics, is as absurd as assuming that the effects of a hot climate upon a culture could be limited to tropical diseases."

— William Kuhns

The first chapter of Tom Peters' second book, A Passion for Excellence—The Leadership Difference is titled "A Blinding Flash of the Obvious." I don't know if I have ever read a more appropriate beginning to an excellent book. Peters continues his study of the best-run and best-performing American companies in the book, but starts with the fact that it contains nothing of substance that is really new.

I am an optimist by nature. At a younger age my ambitions were not offset by the cynicism of experience. I was always looking for the shortcut or the get-rich-quick scheme. My honest efforts were constantly being diverted by a "secret technique" or a "revolutionary breakthrough." Instead of focusing solely on my job, I spent an inordinate amount of time attempting and searching for the "true" shortcuts that worked every time.

I am now the personification of the saying that, "Cunning and old age will beat youth and enthusiasm every time." There is not a blind alley I have not visited. There is not a technique I haven't tried. And there is no guaranteed shortcut to success. There is luck, but that's in a totally different realm. I manage salespeople who, I imagine, are drawn to work for me because I tell them I can teach them how to be successful in sales. Unfortunately, they are like our children who fail to listen to the advice we give them and insist on making the same mistakes we made in our youth. Salespeople listen just long enough to learn what they should do; then they decide they, too, will find the ever-illusive shortcut to success.

Life is not rocket science. There is no complicated secret to success. Getting rich is relatively easy, but it is not quick. Nor is there a shortcut to the process. It is too bad that our society has adapted the lottery mentality where immediate satisfaction is still not quick enough. Every business plan must surpass the last. Every investment must be better than the last. Every promise must be more fulfilling than the one before. Soon everyone is looking for that shortcut to success, and far too many people not only believe it exists, but they begin to depend upon it.

Doing the right thing because it is the right thing to do, delivering more value than is expected, only promising things you know you can deliver, and delivering everything you promise are the blindingly obvious laws of success. When we begin to shortcut, we find we must work harder, and we must work more. Many people challenge these laws every day only to find that when they violate them, the effort required to make up for a missing element is more costly than just surrendering to the get-rich-slowly rules.

I recommend to my salespeople that they avoid useless effort. By that I mean that they should not get sidetracked by nonproductive diversions. They should stick with the procedures that, over time, are proven to work. But to a person, they think they can sell a lesser product for more, or they believe doing half of something will garner the same result as completing the entire process. Even more frustrating is that we as a culture believe in the lottery mentality so much that we conscientiously repeat processes that we know have failed, hoping to they will turn out differently because we desire them to do so. Somewhere, there is money to be made as a bookmaker for videotaped replays. With as many business executives as there are that bet on different outcomes from repeating business processes, there just has to be as great a market out there as there were for bets on last year's Super Bowl.

OK, so I hope I have made my point about depending upon shortcuts that do not work. Another obvious fact is that if you want to grow, you must invest. In my experience, I have not seen long-term growth come from continual cuts. Even if the investment of capital is not expanded, there must be an investment of intellect, effort or improved skill.

I repeatedly see new people making advertising decisions. They are hired by the same people who fired the last person making advertising decisions. These new people follow the guidelines of the people who hired them, as I suppose did those who were fired. Here we go again, repeating failing efforts but thinking a new person executing it will change the consequence. If you want to grow your business, invest. Invest money, effort and/or increased quality. Do something essentially different. But do not believe that a different person performing the same ineffective process will generate new results.

Go back to doing the right thing because it is right, delivering more value than is expected and only promising what you can deliver, then delivering what you promise. Growing your business is not as hard as it may seem. Too many businesses get away from why they went in into business in the first place. Most started out because they felt they could provide a better product or better service than others in the business. Eventually, it comes down to money. But when money becomes the only goal, you'd better hope you are an investment banker where money is the product. Otherwise, striving for only for the money will cause it to evade you.

Your goal should be to serve your customers better than your competition. A business should strive to amaze and astound its customers. Give more than is expected and customers will be loyal; customers will come to you, and you will force the competition to play your game. Notice that customers gladly pay a premium for high-quality products. The premium pricing allows for increased quality, improved service, as well as more generous margins. It is only when a company allows its product to become a commodity, by failing to differentiate the product that it becomes purchased solely on price, which drives profits down. Do I even need to mention that a goal of advertising is to differentiate products, add value, and when appropriate, position the product's premium pricing?

Leadership is not only a characteristic of individuals, it also defines products. Taking the leadership position means doing the things everyone would expect a leader to do. "Do the right things because they are the right things to do." Leadership is an existential act of courage. It is stepping into a role of what is the right thing to do from not being there. Being the leader is not a process. It isn't something that evolves. One moment you are not a leader, and the next moment you are. It is a courageous step forward into setting an example for others to aspire to. Frankly, it is easy to envision what a leader should look like and should do. It takes real commitment and courage to do it.

Companies that lead, win. Everyone loves the leader. Everyone loves the winner. Everyone assumes that leading companies are No. 1 in all categories. The market leaders are not always the biggest, nor even the best. They are the ones that consistently set the example of doing the right thing because it is the right thing to do. Leadership affords profits and benefits beyond its market share. It is a coveted place to be, and one that every honest company should aspire to. There can only be one in the top position, but many can be working to get there.

Let me make one last point. I am not talking about being perfect. Perfection is an admirable trait, but it is also a great step toward bankruptcy. I am talking about being "better," not perfect. This reminds me of a story: Two friends were out on a hunting adventure in the woods, far from any type of civilization. After several hours of walking, they both accidentally fell down the side of the hill, losing their guns and tumbling down in front of a grizzly bear's den. The noise of their fall woke up a giant grizzly bear that stuck its head out and looked at the two defenseless hunters lying on the ground. Frightened, one hunter turned to his friend and said; "How are we going to outrun the bear?" The other jumped up and said, "I don't have to, I just need to outrun you."

Make sure in your evaluation that you outrun your competition. You cannot afford bias or poor judgment. The market is as cruel as a hungry grizzly bear and offers no more remorse, so do outrun your competition by the market's standards. Become the leader but don't wait to be perfect.

Uniquely You

*"Every man has his own destiny; the only imperative is to
follow it, to accept it, no matter where it leads him."*

— Henry Miller

I love to play golf. I spend probably more time doing so than I'd like
to admit. Fridays after work, I'll stop at the country club on my way
home to get in nine holes. The weekends that I am not traveling, I rush
through my Saturday chores and errands to see if I can spend some
time late in the afternoon on the driving range. I have a standing tee
time with my brother, my uncle and a family friend very early every
Sunday morning. And my company has a Monday afternoon golf
league with twenty-eight regulars and me serving as the commissioner
for the eleventh consecutive year.

It was not always that way. In fact when I was younger and had
little time, I thought anyone chasing a little white ball with a stick was
approaching sanity from the wrong direction. But as I matured and
became cultured and more civilized, I learned to embrace the challenge
and nuances offered by golf. I'm not what most people would call a
very good golfer, but in this last year I have learned to love the game
and consider myself an avid player.

In his book Extraordinary Golf: The Art of the Possible, golf pro
Fred Shoemaker says that the culture around the game is based in
something being wrong. To improve your game you must believe that
you are doing something incorrectly. To improve you must "fix" what
you are doing. Improvement comes as you eliminate your mistakes one
by one, until you have perfected your game. The problem is you never
totally eliminate all of the variables so you end up in a perpetually

dissatisfied state with something left to fix. Something is still wrong. Shoemaker suggests that this very culture is what robs golfers of experiencing the full richness of the game.

Shoemaker contends that every golfer has his own perfect swing, not a swing where you move your body to simulate the swing of Tiger Woods or Phil Mickelson. You have your own swing and the innate ability to perform at an extraordinary level. By becoming aware of your unique swing and focusing on this awareness, you allow yourself to make minor adjustments without thinking, similar to "learning" to control your balance in riding a bicycle. This method employs a human's almost perfect learning system and allows you to enjoy the game of golf "naturally."

So what does extraordinary golf have to do with advertising? I believe the approach to advertising should be similar. Every company has its own unique characteristics. The secret is to be your company and be it as well as you can be. Don't aspire to the standards or results of other advertisers, but aspire to what is possible for your company. In essence, be the best possible you that you can be.

Take a moment to give yourself credit for the ground you've gained. Every new customer is a victory. Enjoy each one. Remember that you can only make a difference one person at a time and the best way to enjoy your business is the very same way. Too often in the scramble to grow our businesses, we don't acknowledge the incremental progress toward our overall goal.

Maybe it is possible to have a larger goal for our business than making money. What if amazing our customers every day was our goal and making money was just one of those things that happened along the way? Focusing your efforts on creating amazing experiences with each customer and seeing them truly enjoy working with your company and/or your products certainly seems more fulfilling than finding a way to get money from people. And this goal fulfills one of mankind's deepest needs: making a difference.

Gaining more enjoyment from your business or vocation can be as easy as broadening the reasons you do what you do. Having a cause or mission larger than making money gives people the kind of career most aspire to have. We all want to do something meaningful and fulfilling, but our perspective is that we do what we do to make money. At some point in our careers, we allowed ourselves to forget our bigger motives and switched from living a mission to having a job.

I caution you not to do this as a trick or gimmick. Insincerity here is worse than not having any goals at all. Your customers will see through it and the process will be less satisfying for you than just being honestly greedy. Honestly, you do not need to fake it. Each of us began our careers with a strong desire to make a difference. We each have a unique blend of talents unmatched by anyone else in the world. Therefore we all have our very own approach to serving the world. Like a golf swing, our approach is uniquely ours and ours alone. Do not try to be anyone other than who you are. Let your uniqueness shine through. Your customers will love you and you will be far happier.

Those of you who own your company can project your unique personality and mission through your advertising message. Done with sincerity, your messages will inspire and motivate customers. Those who work for others can still share your uniqueness in how you advertise and market your business. Remember that it is far more fun and often more profitable to serve customers than it is to try to make money.

Advertising can be an expression as well as a tool. It can -- and in my opinion should --reflect the being of your business. People react more strongly to who you are than to what you have to sell or what you say. Let your image speak volumes about the being of your company. The goal or mission you choose is more compelling than the price point you offer. Your company's unique personality has more charisma than a 10% discount. Allow your customers to experience the richness of your company, similar to the richness of golf that is experienced by Fred Shoemaker's students.

The average person develops skills as they grow, inevitably using those skills to react to events and situations that befall them. They call these reactions to arbitrary events living a life. Extraordinary people create a vision, intentionally develop the skills, evoke the conditions and orchestrate the events to have their future unfold as they have purposefully designed it. I call that living a life!

What is the real competition for our products?

"You can fool all the people all the time if the advertising is right and the budget is big enough."

— Joseph E. Levine

When I have spare time, I treasure it like never before. Even though statistics tell us that we have more leisure time than at any other time in human history, the perception is that we are all rushed. Compared to just a few years ago, each of us has more available time to fill with whatever activities we choose, yet there is an almost universal complaint about being overworked or not having enough time.

The variable here is stress. Just a few decades ago, far eastern countries had great leaps of productivity and made strides against the United States economy because they were producing more for less. The American economy and business model responded by pushing our own productivity levels. Each year we pushed for more from individual workers and added automation to further enhance productivity. Year after year American business expected double digit increases.

During the 1990s, the RCA manufacturing plant in Marion, Indiana had a year of hiring freezes, while simultaneously pushing production to higher levels. For the first time in the plant's history, line workers reported incomes of over $100,000 because of all of the overtime they were allowed for the production increase. The next year, with even more demand for increased production, the same plant had fewer six figure incomes, and absenteeism was one of the biggest HR problems of the facility.

Workers had reached their limit. They chose less money with more leisure time over making more money and having less personal time. This phenomenon appeared in several different ways across the country; the American worker been pushed to the limits of physical and mental capacities.

About the same time marketers noticed a change in response to typical marketing strategies. The American public was changing. Thomas Connellan in his 1997 book, Inside the Magic Kingdom: Disney's Seven Secrets to Success, explains how the Disney organization competes in the customer service arena. Disney considers every encounter the customer has as a form of competition.

Share of mind –share of time, consumer stress has invaded their mindset to such a degree that even though we do have more time, it is not as satisfying because we are anticipating the stress of future events, such as work and other commitments that are filling our lives today.

One of the Mickey's biggest customer service secrets is believing he competes with everyone. According to Disney, every outside influence competes for 'share of mind – share of time' with each and every consumer. If your customer service experience is better with FedEx, then Disney loses a share of mind to that competitor. It is easy to see why the "Kingdom" has extraordinary customer service. When they talk about world class service, it is not service within the limited category of the world's amusement parks or vacation destinations. Disney considers the entire world as it competitor. No wonder the standards are so high for this company.

Do we in the craft industry understand that our biggest competitor is not another craft company, but the public library, a community theater or a local charitable organization where our potential customer volunteers, investing a portion of their all-too-valuable leisure time? How do we compete with these altruistic causes and win?

If today's consumers are so stressed that they jealously guard their leisure time, what does that say to those of us in the craft industry who market leisure time activities? How do we compete with other consumer diversions? What can we do to get our 'share of mind – share of time'? Most importantly, how do we sell our products to a public that truly believes it has less available time than it really does? We all know that telling the customer he/she is wrong will do little to win his/her heart. Since the consumer's perception is their reality, how can we appeal to their perception to increase our sales results?

The best way is to be aware of what pulls our prospective customers. Why do they guard their time, and what type of emotional reward is required for them to 'spend' this prized commodity? Disney understands and respects the value placed on individual leisure time like few other companies in the world. Their results are a tribute to this understanding.

The best customer service is not a goal to be achieved someday for Disney. It is a commitment for right now or not at all. In the Disney mindset, "being the best" is not belonging to a group, "best" is a singular position at the very end of a spectrum. For many others, "best" is a relative term and leads, unfortunately to relative results.

The Craft Yarn Council of America, a trade group, does consumer research on the use of yarn in the craft industry. Some years ago, they released a study reporting that nearly seventy percent of American women knew how to crochet or knit. Interestingly, only a small portion of those who know how to crochet or knit actually spend time doing it. This is our problem.

When I entered this industry, my mother mentioned that she had not crocheted nor knitted anything in twenty years. It was my association with the needle arts that brought her back to active status in our segment of the craft market.

"Crafts – Discover life's little pleasures." the campaign used industry-wide a few years ago was a step in the right direction. But it did not, I fear, have the clarity of Disney's understanding in just how vast the competition to our efforts really is.

We need to enroll our prospects in using our products. To do so, it is useful to understand just who we are competing with. Sure, guy who makes products similar to yours is a competitor. The bigger competitor vies for 'share of mind – share of time' with things that appear to offer a safer haven than we do. It may be a movie, a book, even a nap on a winter's afternoon. If we can compete with what our customers do to escape stress, and become a viable alternative, the guy across the street is the least of our worries.

Recycle? I don't even own a bike

"It takes a big idea to attract the attention of consumers and get them to buy your product. Unless your advertising contains a big idea, it will pass like a ship in the night. I doubt if more than one campaign in a hundred contains a big idea."

— David Ogilvy

That was pretty much my reaction when I was first introduced to the term "recycle" in the mid-'70s. The conservation movement found me a typical capitalist consumer, buying disposable-material items as quickly as I could and figuratively throwing my refuse out the window of my car. At the time, I was in the broadcast industry and recycling quickly became a hot topic. We were introduced to the concepts of global warming, the loss of rain forests, and the depletion of the ozone layer in the atmosphere. These things gave all of us pause to think about our personal responsibility toward our planet.

Earth day and other events were organized to publicize the planet's inevitable future if drastic measures were not taken to save us from our own overindulgence. Many great things emerged from these times, the Environmental Protection Agency, standards for gas mileage and automotive emissions. Many major corporations were exposed as polluters and were given huge fines for indiscriminately dumping harmful substances into landfills and rivers. The steps taken in the initial years of the movement are still paying dividends to all of us.

As time has gone on, the story has evolved, the research is more extensive, and mankind's impending devastation is even closer. The vocabulary, too, has expanded and evolved. Now "environmentally safe" is "green." And the cycle begins anew with a solid core of activists joined by additional generations full of passion, intent and verve to encourage us to change our habits and save the earth.

Say what you will about the claims that mankind is capable of destroying the earth. With a belief in a superior being, I find it supremely arrogant to believe mankind could destroy such a magnificent creation of divine design. Certainly divine intent could render our efforts fruitless in a near instant with a volcano eruption or a giant meteor crash. Regardless, one thing is certainly true: the passion of those who do believe in our power to destroy, and to save, the earth. And as businesspeople we cannot afford to ignore their pleas nor their insistence that we produce eco-friendly products and be responsible stewards of the planet.

Green products are everywhere. At the winter Craft and Hobby Association trade show last February, many companies offered green products. Several companies launched entire lines of environmentally friendly products. Roughly 10 percent of Americans now actively seek out products that are green, i.e. safer for the environment. All things being equal, most of the other 90 percent can be persuaded to follow the practice of conscious buying. In the same way that people have learned to consult the nutrition information now available on every package of food, consumers are beginning to be aware that they can make wiser choices that agree with their social consciences. Through advertising and celebrity endorsements, it is becoming fashionable to be "green."

Recently, many companies have found it very profitable to market exclusively to women after it was discovered that women decide or influence over 85 percent of all purchases. Those who were not marketing exclusively to women are saying, "Why not?" Similarly, those companies that have products that are eco-friendly by design or even by accident should be promoting this product advantage to everyone. With 10 percent of the general population actively seeking green products, it is easy to assume that that percentage would increase with a craft audience made up of predominantly females. Green product features are one more way to invite consumers to find your company special. Those who are passionate about the environment certainly will do so.

My company recycles and is a responsible corporate citizen. In our offices, we have special containers for aluminum cans, paper and other recyclable waste. We collect, grind up and put into bails, used publication paper that is collected for recycling. Even though our product is printed we are responsible about the environment. We limit our print overruns to reduce the amount of paper waste. Our newsstand business is small because of the associated waste of non-sold magazine issues. We have in the planning paperless digital issues to serve more readers with less paper waste. The ink we use and the printing plant where our publications are printed are environmentally safe. We are a responsible corporate citizen. Yet, even we fail to promote this strategic advantage to separate ourselves from other less-responsible and less-reputable publishers.

I believe that today's environmentalists are interested in the companies behind the products. Like the initiatives practiced by my company, many manufacturers have policies that are kind to our planet. Each of these initiatives is of interest to a growing number of consumers. They provide reasons beyond a product's features to do business with a particular company. A larger portion of today's consumers want to know what others are doing to protect the earth. But even though these actions are valid and enticing, they are undervalued unless used. It is time for many in the craft industry to jump on the bandwagon and go green. Large corporations, major media companies and even political parties have gone green in an attempt to woo the public. Taking a stance that is already successful for others is not taking too much of a chance, and it could actually broaden your potential.

You cannot be too careful with today's consumers. Those who care deeply about the environment could be wearing jeans and a sweater, or a suit and tie. They could be driving a minivan or a hybrid SUV. They may take out recyclables or only buy biodegradable products and containers. On the street or in the boardroom the people who care about the environment look the same as the ones who don't. Can you afford not to invite them to buy your eco-friendly offerings? Can you afford not to inform them about the efforts your company and your employees make to protect our planet? Go green and let everyone know.

It is that time of year again.

*"The great enemy of the truth is very often not the lie --
deliberate, contrived and dishonest, but the myth, persistent,
persuasive, and unrealistic. Belief in myths allows the comfort
of opinion without the discomfort of thought."*

— John F. Kennedy

It is budget time, that time of the year when advertisers are not ready
to move forward and salespeople need space commitments for the first
of the year issues. It is an age-old problem. Advertisers are planning
next year's new and greatest campaigns. Their bosses are expecting sales
increases, expense reductions and fabulous margins. Advertising people
need to move forward with January and February issues, those that will
be distributed at trade shows, the same ones that give an indication of
how the year's sales might fare.

We all expect it to be different this year just like our expectations
at this time last year. Yet very few of us stretch to do anything new
and different. The fact is, many of us are so busy we typically "cut
and paste" last year's initiatives and update them just enough to look
different. We are so busy making a living that we do not have the time
to get rich. Rather than think about (and I mean using your head and
really thinking) new and innovative ways to have our products appeal
to customers, we do what we've always done.

I cannot tell you the number of advertising prospects I have dealt
with over the last 25 years who told me they were going to add my
publications to their budget for the upcoming year. They genuinely
mean it. They even ask me to prepare specific proposals for them. But
when the pressure is on to limit "out of control spending," they, like

every other well-meaning prospect in past years, cut and paste last year's budget. After all, the boss approved it last year, why wouldn't he do it again this year?

If you think I am wrong, compare your advertising habits over the past three to five years. Unless something significant has happened in your company (and isn't that what we hope our ad campaigns will do – make something significant happen?), your budget and expenditures are probably pretty consistent with previous years. This reminds me of the saying, "If you always do what you have always done, you will always get what you have always gotten." And we wonder why we don't make giant strides moving our companies forward with our advertising initiatives. Is it any wonder things don't improve when we replicate efforts from a period that generated mediocre results?

I hope everyone, advertisers and salespeople alike, will take a little extra time this year to put together innovative campaigns, creative media placements and special features that will entice customers and build sales for us all. Caving into the pressure to reduce budgets when forecasts are increased does no one good. If last year's $250,000 budget didn't get the job done, why would anyone expect to make it on $225,000 in the coming year? But more often than not, this is the reality we all face each year during budget time.

Just Ask Who?

"Life isn't about waiting for the storm to pass. It's about learning to dance in the rain."

— Anonymous

Over the years, I have been introduced to many different ways to focus advertising messages. One of my first and most effective lessons was to learn about psychographics. A combination of geographic, demographic and lifestyle data, psychographic studies collate different personality styles into five separate and distinct buying groups. The members of each group have similar characteristics which lend themselves to five different psychological advertising approaches. These models have held true over several decades and can be very helpful in creating copy points and approaches to marketing products.

Understanding psychographics early in my career helped me tremendously in crafting advertising messages for my clients. Like other lessons I learned from positioning, guerilla marketing and neurolinguistics, psychographics gave me new ways to effectively communicate with potential customers.

My first wife, a former president of the National Speakers Association was in high demand on the speaking circuit espousing effective communication between men and women by understanding the subtle but key personality differences in the sexes. In 1992, John Gray published his first Mars and Venus book on relationships, Men are from Mars and Women and from Venus. Creating marketing messages based upon gender instantly gained popularity.

Gender-based marketing of non-gender-based products gained greater popularity as the influence of females on purchasing patterns became more widely recognized. Most marketers now know that anyone, male or female, rarely makes a purchasing decision in a vacuum. Most often, the major influence is carried by the female

Many of my advertising years were spent in broadcast industry. From 1976 through 1995, the top demographic category routinely picked for nationally advertised products was women 25-54 years old. Packaged goods manufacturers have been aware for many years of the influence carried by the woman of the household.

In 2003, Mary Lou Quinlan published the book, Just Ask a Woman – Cracking the Code of What Women Want and How They Buy. This book is a great primer for anyone who markets products to a broad base of customers. If you are marketing your product to more than a remote group of tribesmen in a tropical jungle, you can bet that a female is going to have influence on the buying decision. In fact, if your product promotion does not target a female audience, you may want to consider making some changes in the way you do business.

Today, women buy or influence the purchase of 85 percent or more of what is sold, as reported by www.ewowfacts.com. That is a large market to own. As a matter of fact, I cannot imagine anyone not wanting to sell to this market. In recent years, larger companies have revised and revamped their approach to customers with the understanding that if you sell to women, the rest of the market will follow.

Mary Lou Quinlan points out that today's woman is pulled in so many directions that she is continually stressed out. She feels the needs to "have it all," and be the super mom and super wife that we see on TV. This stress to excel outside the home and the need to be all for their families has created an entirely new consumer. Do you think there is not stress among woman? Fifty-five percent of mothers with children younger than twelve months have jobs in addition to being a mother. Not only is stress and lack of time a constant companion but there is no end in sight for the woman who wishes to "have it all." You must contend with this new reality if you plan to sell you product to this market.

In the craft industry we experienced a soft market last year as relief efforts from Hurricane Katrina and escalating gasoline prices squeezed family budgets during the second and third quarters of the year. The woman of the house, our primary customer, sacrificed purchases she usually made for herself to compensate for the squeeze on the family budget. Household budgets mostly adjusted by year's end, but a noticeable slow-down occurred. Even today's most sophisticated advertisers could pay more attention to the business benefits of helping mothers take care of their families.

Marketers who have not updated their thinking show today's woman as rushed, harried and out of control. This is not the image that you potential consumer wishes to have of herself. She has had her negative experiences with marketers and now has revised who she trusts and how she evaluates products and services. She has her own network of advisors and often turns to this network when looking for advice or approval for a purchasing decision. Understanding her network and this decision-making process will lead to not only selling her but also the network she advises. Shunning her can lead to being shunned by her entire network.

Today's woman is a complex and unique consumer. In less than four years, she is expected to control 60% of the country's wealth. She already influences 85% of consumer purchases. Understanding what makes her tick, why she is evolving, and how to speak to her real and emotional needs may well be the key to success for your business. Relying on practices of the past could easily spell doom and gloom for marketers who think it worked before, it will work again.

From John Gray's Mars and Venus series to Mary Lou Quinlan's Just Ask a Woman, seek expert advice on the subject. If you are a woman, you may be too close to the reality to see it clearly. If you are a man, you need a perspective outside of your personal experience. You want to know not only who buys your product, but all of the inbred, cultural and societal influences that mold her today.

Personal note: For all of you who so kindly responded to the issue of ADvice that mentioned John Robinson, my boss who recently passed away, thank you. I appreciate your kind words and thoughts. Our birthday was February 11, the day after the issue was published. Being a Saturday, John would have emailed me at home rather than call and worry about bothering my time with my family. The response the issue received made it a special birthday indeed.

A brand you can love

*"Strategy and timing are the Himalayas of marketing.
Everything else is the Catskills."*

— Al Ries and Jack Trout

This morning I read a wonderful article about branding by Al Ries of Trout and Ries from the classic advertising book Positioning: The Battle for Your Mind fame. Ries modernizes his concept and chimes in with the old "make your customers fall in love with you" routine. He compares brand loyalty to being in love with your spouse, or being politically correct, your significant other. In the comparison we may readily admit there are better products available to fulfill a need, but most people are remarkable about maintaining the stance of "love the one you're with."

Marketers never seem to fully appreciate the intangible territory of brand loyalty, whereas ad people spend a great deal of their time in that realm. Marketers seem only interested in the here and now. It's the old "what have done for me today" mentality. I would hate to be married to a marketer, because I would be afraid that if I had an off day, I" be replaced by a newer, more efficient model. Fortunately for me, my wife is more like an ad person; she appreciates me for the glow of my past performance as well as the considerable intangible value of the totality of my achieved tasks over the years.

Come to think of it, many of us would hate to be held to the marketing standards to which we hold our products. Ries makes the point in his article that being "in love with" is not the same as "loving." Something that you just "love," you can still let go. Being "in love" with something prevents you from considering that eventuality. To let it go, you must first fall out of love with it.

In masterful style, Ries completes his article by tying his observation back into what we all know and appreciate Al Ries for -- positioning. He makes the point that people don't stick with Coca Cola because they love it. They are In Love with Coca Cola, because it is The Real Thing, The Original, The First and The Only in the minds of branded customers.

Branding's current reputation is an indescribable lack of accountability that at one time was associated with advertising. Today, the word "advertising" is used in more general terms, and the discipline of "branding" has fallen into disrepute among those "in the know." But brand loyalty is the difference between Coca Cola and Cheryl's Cola. It is the difference between Kleenex and Regal 2-Ply Facial Quality Tissues. Branding is the investment that increases today's return on sales, as well as the value of what has not even been sold yet.

In a rough economy, I would much rather be dependent upon a branded product than one marketers strictly sold for margins. An old sales adage is, "When price is introduced before value is established, price becomes the controlling factor." It could be said about branding that, "When features are stressed without the brand being built, the next additional feature wins the sale." Remember, it is easy to beat a purely marketed product after it has been pitched -- just add a feature or undercut the price by a dime. It is nearly impossible to outsell a product that people are in love with. Even when you alienate your customer base by coming out with "New Coke," a well-branded product can recover from a grand marketing error and still survive.

In a previous chapter of this newsletter I wrote about market share being available at half price or better during economic times of stress. Branding deserved to be a portion of that discussion. Great opportunities abound and are around all of us, even as you read this newsletter. They do not look the way we expect them to look. Great opportunities rarely do show up as expected -- so many times we walk right by them. But a couple of years or just a few months from now, each of us will see or run across the result of something that someone with courage is doing today, and say, "I wish I would have done that."

I wish I were smart enough to recognize all of those opportunities now (or even just one of them!) and were courageous enough to say "count me in too." But extraordinary success is not meant for all of us; the purpose for many of us in life is to be part of the masses, or heaven forbid, to be the example of what not to do.

Ries finishes his article by asserting that the first established product of a type is usually the one people fall in love with. And until they give up that position voluntarily or by default, there is virtually nothing anyone can do to win over it. I agree with his assertion, but I would add the caveat that during difficult times like now, those companies that have enjoyed the luxury of customers being in love with them are pulling back on their branding dollars and allowing those loyal customers to fall out of love with them. When they do, don't market to them, advertise to them. Build a brand of your own that they can love.

My Way

There is a parable about the man walking along the edge of a mountain. He stumbles and falls over a cliff only to grab a root that is sticking out. As he hangs over a large precipice he calls out for help. With the passing of precious minutes his grip begins to tire and he prays out loud. "Dear Lord, please help me. I don't want to die. I'll do anything you ask, just please save me." After a minute a voice rumbles from the cliff above that says, "I'm here and I'll save you." The man says, "Thank you, thank you. I don't want to die." From above the voice says, "Please follow my instructions completely and I will save you as soon as you do." "Okay," said the man. "What do you want me to do?" "Let go." The voice says...., after hearing this, the man queried, "Is there anyone else up there?"

So it goes with advertising. We all want the results of advertising, yet none of us want to advertise. Each month I encounter several companies who are "changing our strategy and putting our funds into a more accountable means of increasing sales." It is inevitable that people will look for a better way. And who am I to point out that if a better way existed, advertising would be obsolete and the person who found the better way would be richer than Bill Gates? But try as I might, I cannot restrain myself from pulling out my soapbox and more people than you would imagine think I am the idiot.

I sincerely hope that one day I will be the advertising guy who runs into that special person who actually does find the complete alternative to advertising. Maybe he'll be so excited about the growth of his own business that he'll let me be his disciple, carrying the message of his secret formula to generate sales without asking people to buy. Then I'll be richer than Bill Gates. That's wishful thinking on my part, and I'm doubtful it will ever happen.

Business can survive without advertising. It happens every day. Seldom do you see these as the top businesses in their category. More often than not they are the smaller proprietorships where the owner does the majority of the work and in the end are not much different than if that person was working for a company: same income, higher liability. In other instances, advertising costs are disguised, as in paying extraordinary rent for a great location. Or prices are discounted to such a degree that they serve as the advertising. Most companies spend advertising funds to stay in business; they just don't know they are doing so.

"Is there anyone else up there?" Why do you suppose the man asked that? It's fear of the unknown. It is the same reason that reasonably intelligent business people look me straight in the eye and tell me that they are going to do what nobody in the history of business has done: find a cheaper, more reliable alternative to advertising. Again, if this were possible, advertising would have been obsolete many years ago. Fear of spending money, of not getting a return on their investment, and of not being up to the challenge is why businessmen declare they will find a better way.

The best that most businesses can do is to hire competent advertising people, give them space for creativity and support the advertising function adequately. Competent advertising people are not college students working part-time. Creativity cannot happen within a rigid structure. And support is more than "Here's a thousand bucks, let's try it for a month and see what happens." The value of advertising's return is in proportion to its investment in dollars and intellect. But the investment must be balanced. Too much intellect without dollars will yield no more than too many dollars with little intellect.

Today's top advertising professionals make more money than the businessman who refuses to advertise. I can't compare top advertising men to top businessmen, because top businessmen do advertise. Again, the majority of today's top executives know that it takes advertising to grease the wheels of industry. How often do we see that a commitment to advertising goes hand in hand with a successful business? Why do top advertising executives earn so much? Because they are committed to the proposition that advertising will work. Based on research, trial and error, and years of experience, they have eliminated much of what doesn't work. This leaves them with insights into what does work and they win more than they lose. You will not reach this point if you are not committed to finding a way to make advertising work. And remember, nobody has found a solution outside of advertising strong enough to eliminate the need to advertise.

My grandmother always told me that you cannot have a marriage if divorce is an option. As long as you have on foot outside of the circle you are never truly committed to finding a solution during tough times. An escape clause, such as a divorce, makes it too convenient to take the "easy way out." So it is with advertising, with those who are fearful of competing in the advertising arena and vowing to find the workable alternative. Their lack of commitment to advertising gives them an easy way out. But it is short-sighted because they falsely believe that they can do what nobody has yet done.

I am humbled by this industry. Often I am amazed at how simplicity itself can claim the day and achieve brilliant results for a company. Other times it amazes me at the complexity needed to achieve minute goals in a moving matrix of market competition, economic firestorms and cultural changes. But I am most offended by the smugness of those who scoff at advertising, suggesting that they will do what no man before them has done, and looking down their nose at me while stating so in full confidence. Why can't they just say "Is there anyone else up there?"

Your online store

"Lack of will power has caused more failure than lack of intelligence or ability."

— Flower A. Newhouse

Years ago I worked with mass merchandisers and the grocery industry. I found that retailers -- good retailers -- work very hard and usually with strong reasons. There are times when I must remind myself of that when I face the woefully inadequate customer service in our retail industry, which is quickly defining the decline in American capitalism. But then I remember that in spite of the great strategic minds behind many retail operations, their plans are executed by minimum-wage employees that receive little or no training.

My career includes 20-plus years in the broadcast industry. I was in radio when AM stereo technology was being pushed. In the 1980s, FM radio listeners dominated the broadcast spectrum, and AM radio stations were losing revenue. Transmitting AM radio signals in stereo was supposed to equalize the popularity between AM and FM broadcast bands. What the inventors and promoters of AM stereo failed to take into account was that, at the time, most AM radio listeners were in cars and locations where the speakers were cheap and not made to deliver the sound fidelity that the AM stereo process promised. As a result, AM stereo never received the acclaim that the technology really deserved. The technology in essence died because of a poor delivery system.

Mass merchandisers often suffer from missing links in their delivery systems. Early in my advertising career I witnessed a major promotion being sold to the Hook's Drugstore chain in Indianapolis. At the time, the chain dominated the market with 75 to 100 locations. The promotion involved giving out free tickets to every store visitor, each with individual serialized numbers. Every two hours the major radio station in the area would read out one of the serialized numbers. The person holding the ticket with the number could call the station and win exotic prizes that included trips, hot tubs, jewelry, tickets to sporting and entertainment events, and ultimately several automobiles. The promotion cost nearly half a million dollars and was a total bust because nobody from Hook's Drugstore corporate office bothered to explain the promotion to the cashiers charged with handing out the tickets.

A complete understanding the delivery system of your product all the way to a satisfied customer is vitally important for the continued success of your business. The weakest link is often where we make assumptions. Hook's Drugs assumed the cashiers understood that every visitor needed to be given a serialized ticket so they had an opportunity to win the prizes. Sony, one of the developers of early AM stereo assumed a "build it and they will change habits" attitude about how people use AM radio.

As a potential Internet retailer you cannot afford to misunderstand your delivery system from start to finish. You must understand where the flow of the product might encounter constraints. Dr. Eliyahu M. Goldratt's classic book The Goal explores how these seemingly small restrictions to the process can negatively impact overall productivity.

New customers are far more difficult to get than reselling to established customers. Unfortunately, in uncertain times the attrition of our current customer base is much higher because far more customers watch their expenditures and opt out of the market more frequently than when times are stable. This means finding new customers is more important than ever. It's too bad the herd mentality is to stop searching for new customers in good times, because continually seeking new customers enables us to maintain the size of our customer base when business slows. This inaccurate thinking actually contributes to the self-fulfilling prophecy of the business slowdown.

A stronger strategy would be to analyze your product-delivery processes and strengthen every weakness you can find. Invest in customer service to ensure every new customer has a positive experience and is more apt to give you repeat and even referral business.

Online retailers must understand the process by which their online store is discovered. Finding a URL is likely never an accident. A visitor generally comes from another Web site where a banner advertisement is encountered. Often this happens when the visitor is engaged in a site that they frequent. Some of these may be encountered while at work. I do a lot of work online and will occasionally see a banner that interests me personally. I'll click through to see what it is. But, like most of you, I feel guilty indulging myself on company time and rarely spend much time there, often promising myself to revisit on my own time. Does this sound familiar? Research shows a surprising amount of personal shopping and surfing occurs at work.

If this truly happens, what does it tell you about how to design your landing page? Maybe suggesting the visitor bookmark your page for an easy return is a very strong strategy, or perhaps capturing the visitor's e-mail address with permission to send offers is the highest priority, so you can market to them should they fail to revisit. Limiting the options on the landing page will ensure that the visitor will do what you want them to do. After you capture their information, sell them a product, or get them to bookmark your site, you can allow them to access your home page or other pages where the visitor can explore a larger variety options.

An axiom that has served me over the years seems very appropriate here. "Sell the prospect, educate the customer." Until your visitor becomes a customer, or is at least committed by sharing contact information, you run the risk of a wasted effort if you educate them about your products and services. Giving them too much information up front gives them total control in the decision-making process, which is one of the top no-no's in the sales game.

There seems to be a universal desire by newer online retailers to give too many options to new visitors. This unfortunately leads to indecision and fewer completed transactions. It is best to remember that the best invitation to a Web site offers a single benefit. The landing page should first and foremost fulfill that promise of the offer before allowing the visitor to go anywhere else. This one strategy can easily make the difference between success and failure of any online campaign.

Once you achieve your goal with a new visitor then give them access that is to your benefit. Make sure to show them your loss leaders, specials and promotional features. Remember to sell your strengths early and often.

The grocery industry is very wise in its merchandising plan. Think about these items in your grocery store: eggs, milk, juice, coffee, bread, lettuce and bananas. These are the seven "demand" items in a grocery store. Ninety-eight percent of every grocery cart will have one or more of these items in them. Grocers know this, and these items are placed strategically throughout the store. If you think about these seven locations in the grocery where you shop, I'll bet they take you past virtually every nonessential and high-margin impulse item in the place. That is not mistake; it is a very intentional layout designed to get you to pass as many different items as possible, all in the hopes of stimulating additional unplanned sales.

Can you lay out your online store in the same manner? When customers stop in to buy the item you are known for, make sure they get the opportunity to sample and/or buy other items that might carry better margins. Sign them up for an e-newsletter marketing campaign. Figuratively and literally walk them up and down each aisle in an effort to increase their purchases and engagement. Put high-margin impulse items near your shopping cart, offer coupons for add-on purchases just before you get payment information. After they buy, give them a date and reason to return for a future sale or promotion. The very best time to remind them to come back is right after they have made a purchase with you. Automated e-mailed thank-you notes are more appreciated than you can imagine.

Remember that excellent customer service is a small cost compared to new-customer acquisition cost. "To amaze the customer" used to be part of every associate's job description at Macy's. Nordstrom similarly prides itself on unique customer service above and beyond the customer's expectation. The dollars spent on superior service does more for your company's reputation and customer retention than about anything else. Stepping up customer service when others are sure to be following the herd and cutting back is an easy way to stand head and shoulders above the crowd. And isn't that what we all want in the end?

Human beings want to be acknowledged. High-tech environments like the Internet perform the best when they avail high-touch features such as tailored customer service and direct interface with those who can answer questions. The local natural-gas company is now offering online chats every Thursday evening from 7 until 8 p.m. with customers wishing to learn ways to economize on their heating bills. This is not an overly expensive outreach to customers, but it is a convenient and unique customer-service outreach that is already paying off for the gas company. Maybe your business could do something like this too.

The future of magazines

"People who soar are those who refuse to sit back, sigh and wish things would change. They neither complain of their lot nor passively dream of some distant ship coming in. Rather, they visualize in their minds that they are not quitters; they will not allow life's circumstances to push them down and hold them under."

— Charles R. Swindoll

In the mid-1990s the Internet became available to the consuming public, and with it came a transformation in the manner that information is distributed. Prior to this transformation, knowledge was power. After the Internet explosion, access became power. No longer do you have to be knowledgeable. The Internet has become the great equalizer. It gives anyone access to virtually any information on any subject with the click of a mouse. It is truly amazing the details you can uncover on obscure topics that a short time ago were only known to a select few experts. The ability to surf the Internet has become commonplace. Internet search engines and their technologies are one of today's most valuable business investments.

Many felt that advent of the Internet meant the death of magazines, and there are some that still feel that way. It is a given that the instant access and dynamic programming of the Internet has dramatically transformed not only how we gather information, but it has affected the very manner in which we currently live. The cultural changes in our society because of the Internet are profound. In my lifetime, I cannot think of any other invention that has impacted my life in as many diverse ways as the Internet.

Having a career in advertising, I was extremely excited about the Internet when I personally discovered it in 1994. For the Internet not only provided sight and sound like television, it provided mass-customization through dynamic programming, and it brought the customer to a place where they could not only interact with many products, but could actually complete a purchase transaction. Never in the history of advertising had so many facets been combined in a single location to make purchasing a product as easy as it is today.

Initially many publishers viewed the Internet as the enemy. All too many believed that the Internet would eliminate the need for the printed page. Digital books, e-zines and e-newsletters appeared to have the potential to revolutionize the printing/publishing industry and force the printed page to go the way of the buggy whip. One day the Internet may well replace the printed page. But it will not happen in most of our lifetimes.

Our educational system is still based on printed matter. Our children still write out the ABCs on a chalkboard as a first step in learning. The processes that teach us how to get on in the world are based in paper and ink, both to send and receive communication. It is not likely that a revolution will occur overnight which will eliminate our dependence upon paper and ink.

What the Internet has taught us is mass-customization. Dynamic programming that matches interests and/or predisposed influences to editorial content may well be the best lesson the Internet has given publishers. Finding ways to provide more customized content is now a goal of more and more publishers. Just because assembling a paper-and-ink magazine takes a little more time to produce than the dynamic programming used on the Internet doesn't mean the printing industry will not reinvent itself to remain competitive. One day soon, magazines with a totally personalized table of contents will be a reality.

Even with laptop computers, cellular telephones, Blackberry devices and the iPhone, magazines are still more conveniently portable. Magazines are also disposable (and recyclable) after we consume the information we desire from them. This is not so with today's highly expensive mobile technology. You can fold a magazine to carry it under your arm, fold it again to put into a pocket or roll it into a cylinder to threaten your dog. None of these bonus features apply to a computer, iPhone or Blackberry.

In project-based publishing, readers keep magazines for future use. They want to retain a personal library of projects that they can turn to in the future. Although the Internet has more storage, not one of us feels it is dependable enough to retain information for years and years. The storage turns over too quickly, eliminating the old to make room for the new. As a matter of fact, manuscript publishing has the same shortcomings. Maintaining articles electronically online is not as simple as retaining the hard copy of a magazine.

I do see a day when mass-customization will affect magazine publishing. Subscribers will complete surveys with their subscriptions so records of their editorial preferences will be retained with their subscription records. When a digital printing press pulls their names and addresses, it will also be supplied with data stipulating the type of editorial content to include in a subscriber's specific magazine. Thus each particular magazine would have the possibility of being totally unique for its subscriber. Of course, technology is not quite to the point where individual magazines can efficiently be printed on high-speed printing presses. One day it will be here, and instead of the magazine being replaced by the Internet, it will steal this and similar technology from the Internet to remain a healthy and vibrant industry.

In the meantime, the partnership of the Internet and published magazines remains the strongest combination of mediums for advertising effectiveness. The printed page builds trust with the consumer, and the Internet relies upon that trust to transact business with the consumer. Consumers become comfortable with images branded with magazine ads. They are more likely to click an online ad that has a familiar association. Online advertising becomes less effective unless it continually reinvests in the trust equation by continuing to advertise in print.

Magazines are great forums for exposing consumers to new ideas and concepts. The Internet is a great resource for gaining a deeper understanding of the ideas and concepts you already know about. Rather than being adversarial, magazines and the Internet can be utilized to work hand in hand. Both are engaging mediums because they require attention to use. You must be active to gain information from both magazines and the Internet. This very engagement makes both mediums stronger than television, radio, billboard and many other popular forms of advertising.

Magazines will be around for a long time to come. They are still one of the most affordable advertising vehicles. Magazines are very personal. They accompany us to more rooms in our home, car and on our travels than any other single medium, including cell phones and laptops. Even with recent postal increases, they remain affordable. As a partner to online vehicles, magazines are indispensable and will continue to be so for many years. Far from being the enemy of magazines, the Internet is now one of paper-and-ink publishing's most strategic allies.

Overnight success

"It is better to know some of the questions than all of the answers."

— James Thurber

Oh, how I have worked and toiled to make sure that my career efforts all add up on the positive side of the scales. For years I have been obsessed with delivering more than was expected of me, all to make sure that the single word used to describe my career would be "successful." Like Frank Sinatra, I can sing that the direction I have taken is a little bit "My Way," but putting in the effort was never a question.

I have been lucky in my advertising career by working with some very talented people. A former colleague of mine is the original writer and continues to write for Barney—yes, the purple dinosaur named Barney. He also writes for Sesame Street. Another colleague, who passed away a few years ago, at the height of his career wrote and scored music for several prime-time television shows including Lou Grant as well as over three dozen motion pictures, Black Beauty being one of his most noted scores. I've also worked with some men and women incredibly talented in sales arena. Each of the hardest working was at one time or another declared an "overnight" success as they were discovered by someone for the first time.

In my years of adulthood I have discovered, "overnight success" is an oxymoron and not a true definition. Success requires hard work and applied effort. Those who are perceived to have achieved overnight success did not do so through dumb luck. It is much more likely for a person to be born into prosperity than to have success fall upon his or her shoulders out of purely good fortune, crowning them with success sans the requisite effort.

Sure, there are those who have encountered good fortune. But those who prosper from it have prepared themselves for the very encounter through hard work. Their methodic efforts and hard work have enabled them to see certain events as opportunities rather than situations that just happened. You see, the interpretation of events has so much more to do with success than the uniqueness of the events themselves.

In the terms of some transformational training in which I was once engaged, "Life is a conversation. Your life occurs and unfolds according to the conversation you create about each facet of your experience. Your perception is colored by preconceived expectations. To profoundly change your life, aggressively (and proactively) alter the conversation you hold onto and hence the perceptions you see as fact. If you look for bad, you will find it, even in the hands of goodness. But if you look for good, it will appear to fulfill your expectations even from the depths of hell."

It takes a mental discipline to be able to focus your expectations at a level where life provides you the very opportunity you need to be successful in the normal happenings of each day. But there are scores of people who do it day in and day out. They are not overnight successes. Each of them worked very hard and learned a lot of hard lessons getting to the perspective where life gave them the opportunity they expected.

I doubt that I will achieve "overnight success," since I work in an area where the individual victories are too small, and the communication channels are too fractured for any sizeable group to recognize the result of years of work as some immediate achievement that fell in my lap. But for those folks whom I know have been bestowed with the "you lucky sucker," award, I can say that I have witnessed the kind of effort you have had to invest before the world acknowledged you.

Too bad most novice advertisers expect to become overnight successes, too. If they only knew that such a thing never existed, maybe they would take the approach as described by John Houseman in commercials for Smith Barney some years ago. They will do it the old-fashioned way and "earn it." Too many advertisers expect advertising to work like the lottery. Run an ad and get rich. Oh, if that only worked.

I've tried it enough times in my life to know that it does not. If it did I would have been very rich many years ago.

To "earn it," though, creates a very special feeling. You know where the success came from. You know through trial and error that it was you that generated the success. And finally, you will have the confidence that if you lost it all, you could go out and create it again. You will get none of that from winning the lottery.

It is really too bad that so many folks refuse to roll up their sleeves and find solid answers to the problems they face today. Martin Luther King once said, "Rarely do we find men who willingly engage in hard, solid thinking. There is an almost universal quest for easy answers and half-baked solutions. Nothing pains some people more than having to think." This also applies toward those businesses who wish for success without applying the necessary effort or investment to achieve success. It troubles me to see how many new businesses expect overnight success. When they fail to achieve it, many place the blame on the industry or the economic times. It is becoming more difficult to find those who are willing to work hard and spend the time necessary to learn a business before expecting to becoming success in it.

Several years ago I read the book, The E Myth: Why Most Small Businesses Don't Work and What to Do About It by Michael Gerber. The myth is that small businesses are built and run by entrepreneurs. When you think about it, they really are not. Most small businesses are built and run by people who do a good job at some specialized trade. After years of successfully working for a company or proprietor, they ask themselves, "Why am I making so much money for someone else? Why don't I do this just for me?" He or she then decides to take that skill and open a business practicing that trade. As the business becomes more successful, there needs to be accounting functions, billing and invoicing functions, customer service, advertising/promotion, and certainly sales efforts to maintain a flow of customers. These areas, although necessary for the growth of a company, are certainly not the reason the person started his or her own business. But these functions become more and more necessary for the continuation and success of the business that is itself beginning to run the owner. And the owner, the cornerstone of the business, is the best person to sell the service, and has a vested interest in customer service as well as accounting and managing the profits of the enterprise. The owner is the best person, in terms of understanding his own product, to perform all of these functions. As you can surmise, most entrepreneurs end up spending more time in areas where they lack skills. Eventually they get so far removed from the real reason they went into business for themselves that they become disenchanted by their own dream.

The E Myth is that it is not entrepreneurs that start businesses, but people with specific skills who attempt to become entrepreneurs. Of the few skilled technicians who are successful at becoming entrepreneurs, fewer still find satisfaction in mastering the day-to-day business of running a company or store, when their original goal was just to produce a quality product or service. Is it any surprise that many small business people do not want to advertise? Most do not want to know how. Even fewer want to know why.

There are no overnight successes, only those whose investment into their own preparation has enabled them to seize opportunities that have come along. Many of the opportunities have existed and were in plain sight. What was missing was the ability of the observer to distinguish the opportunities from the background "noise." So-called luck is most correctly defined as when preparation meets opportunity. Preparation does not happen overnight.

Being a skilled technician does not make an entrepreneur. Running a business and having a skill set are entirely different things. Both need practice, knowledge and a desire to succeed in order to flourish. They are not mutually exclusive in business, but neither are they linked.

More often than not, the world will amaze you in its attempt to completely fulfill your expectations. Be not only responsible, but also proactive about the expectations you put into your own mind.

"Sell something more profitable than a low price."

"If you're going to doubt something, doubt your limits."

— Don Ward

The sentence above is a chapter title in the book The 33 Ruthless Rules of Local Advertising, written by my friend Michael Corbett. This is an excellent book for anyone wishing for accountability from their advertising dollar. I call Michael my friend, because not only did he consult a radio-station advertising department I managed, but he also became a coach to me early in my advertising and sales-management career. After his consulting engagement expired, we continue to share success stories for several years until our careers took different turns, and like many such relationships, ours eventually drifted apart. I was very happy to discover Michael's book on Amazon.com a few weeks ago and immediately ordered a copy. I highly recommend it.

Michael is a very competent and focused man who really knows his stuff. He rarely if ever says anything that he cannot back up 100 percent. This might be hard to imagine without knowing Michael, but once you meet him, you will immediately understand why I describe him as being so unique.

In the page and a half chapter titled "Sell something more profitable than a low price," Michael talks about how positioning yourself as a discounted option makes you vulnerable to any competitor willing to offer a slightly larger discount. He also states that only 9 percent of the buyers are strictly motivated by price. In other words, 91 percent of buyers make their purchase decision on a primary factor other than price. Finding some aspect of your business that you can claim as your unique selling proposition is the easiest way to begin building customer loyalty and a base of business. Many companies sell on price because it is easy. It also educates your customer to pricing ranges and makes the prospective customer more price sensitive as a consumer. In the end, you are arming your customers with a buying motive that is not in the long-term interest of your business. And it will probably revisit you when you can least afford it.

When Tom Peters, author of In Search of Excellence, speaks in public he sometimes mentions that he makes far too much money just for telling his audience that in America, if you make a decent product, sell it at a reasonable price, listen to your customers, and fulfill the promises you make to them, you cannot avoid becoming filthy rich. Why? Because, according to Peters, too few companies make adequate products that sell at reasonable prices, or listen to their customers, much less fulfill the promises they make to their customers. It is so rare to find a company committed to serving the customer rather than making money. And it is the small difference between making money and serving the customer's interest at critical "moments of truth" that make all the difference. Part of the 91 percent of buyers mentioned above buy to avoid the known bad service from another company. That creates a huge opportunity for the company that is focused on service.

When I was younger, I lived and worked in the Indianapolis area. I routinely took my clothes to a local dry cleaner twice per week. Everybody there knew my name. Much like the song about the fictional Boston gathering place, Cheers, the employees made me feel like I belonged there when I walked in. If I was running late, not only did they notice, but they would suggest I just leave my cleaning on the counter, and they would write it up after I left and was on my way. Every employee that spoke to me used my name. "Hi John, how's it going this morning? Are you going to the game this weekend?" They would always try to interject something personal with their comments. I really loved the place. They charged about twice as much as the four other dry cleaners I drove past to get to their place of business. I didn't care. The lower-priced competitors forgot my name or worse, they never knew it, and none of them ever made me feel special. Very few businesses have ever given me such personalized service over the years. It took some effort for this company to deliver it, but their effort paid them very well as I, and many of my neighbors, patronized this business religiously for the years I lived in the area.

One of the tips I was given early in my advertising career was to suggest that new advertisers write an ad about how they envisioned their company to be before it opened, not necessarily how the company was currently. The reason was that many businesses were started with a dream of serving customer's needs and becoming more than just a business where people could buy things. As these businesspeople wrote these ads, they got excited about their businesses again and were re-energized to get back to fulfilling the original goals they set out to achieve. These business people were sidetracked by making money, and they lost touch with the bigger reason they opened for business. Those original motives are more apt to attract customers than "10 percent off all inventory." Do not lose site of your original motives. Those goals are inspiring to the 91 percent that buy for reasons other than price.

What is possible? If you were to get reinvigorated about your business and to roll up your sleeves, what is possible for you to do? How far would you take it? What would you do? Sharing your vision is one of the most inspiring things you can do in advertising. People are wired up in such a way that they want to be part of something that is growing and has a future. They intuitively avoid those things that are static and stagnant. Even in conversation people get turned on when discussing the building of something. Is it any wonder that new businesses and businesses that are still evolving feed off of their own momentum to continue that growth? Think about the last time you were excited in a conversation. I'll bet it was conversation about building, developing or creating something new. Seldom does anyone get excited about the status quo or about tearing something down. Sharing the vision for your business and what you hope that means for your customers as well as your employees can be very alluring. There is something to the phrase, "build it and they will come," as long as you share the vision first. If you do, "they," your customers, may very well support your efforts in building it, too.

I've seen several surveys over the years concerning basic buying motivations. While writing today, I could not pull any out of my files for documentation, which is why I led with Michael Corbett's book and his statement of 9 percent buying for price and 91 percent buying for other reasons. Of the studies I remember, price does not rank any higher than number seven in terms of the top reasons people chose a product, service or company. Yet many of us who sell are drawn to price almost every time as a way to validate why someone should buy. Maybe that's because it is the easiest thing to do. Certainly it is easier than creating the ultimate customer experience, providing the highest quality product, or giving more than our customer expects. It may be easier, but it's not as exciting and definitely not as unique.

I have always said, "Anyone can sell anything as long as they lower the price enough." Well, that is not true. I have encountered times when my customers have actually refused something for free. I guess the effort of making a decision was not worth the limited value they saw in my offer. Thanks to Michael Corbett, I can quantify that the price of my products is the prime concern of only a few of my customers. That applies for you and your customers, too.

We the people ...,

"Although advertising is communication unusually candid about its motivation, Americans love to loathe it. As society becomes more complex and opaque, as social processes seem more impersonal and autonomous, and as elites of 'experts' become more annoying, more people are tempted to think that some 'they' is manipulating 'us,' using, among other dark arts, advertising."

— George F. Will

I write this chapter of ADvice as our new president gives his inaugural address. I enjoy these speeches immensely and cannot remember one that failed to inspire me. It is funny because only half of the presidents who have inspired me with their speeches received my vote. It is a great achievement of America's melting pot that "a man, whose father less than 60 years ago might not have been served at a local restaurant, can now stand before you to take a most sacred oath." It must be said of President Obama whether you voted for him or not that he is a charismatic and a well-spoken leader. The question of whether he is able to fulfill the immense expectations the country holds for him is yet to be answered.

Inaugural speeches, on the other hand, are always up for their task and that purpose is to inspire. The vision of a prosperous future these speeches evoke and the rallying plea for sacrifice to achieve unimaginable goals, in the hopes of returning endless prosperity to our children and loved ones, bring together a greater number of constituents than voted for and against the newly elected president. It is a tribute to their wordsmiths that they hold the power to unify both supporters and naysayers alike.

In our immediate future, according to the president, we must roll up our sleeves; put forth the effort and sacrifice to get this country and our economy back on track. I agree. I have been telling everyone that receives this newsletter that sitting back and waiting for the other guy to fix our economy is the wrong thing to do. Irish political philosopher Edmund Burke said, "All that is necessary for the triumph of evil is that good men do nothing." To paraphrase, I say, "All that is necessary for others to take away your business opportunity is to empower the fear in your heart and do nothing."

I see so many businesses currently making the decision to do nothing in the face of uncertainty, when that very uncertainty which motivates them is caused by others doing nothing. Unless and until someone breaks the cycle, nothing will improve. Never has a self-fulfilling prophesy been more apparent, yet still so contagious.

History tells us that our economic situation will change. Since these things have been recorded, each time that business has slowed, it has come back even more robust than before. Fortunes have been made by those few "lucky" companies that created new products, pushed innovation or swam against the tide of playing small during uncertain times. Of course it is more than luck that led to these successes, because they did what others failed to do, they acted. They planned on winning now rather than waiting like the rest until everything was just right before entering the game. Winners have always acted while others have waited.

It is not particularly patriotic to grow your business when times are good. As a matter of fact, getting rich in good times is sometimes seen as self-indulgent, not to mention harder to achieve when everyone is competing to grow. But when our industry, our country and even our free-economy business model is looking for new role models, there is nobody more important than one who is "firm in the knowledge that there is nothing so satisfying to the spirit, so defining of our character, than giving our all to a difficult task."

The president's speech was inspiring. He stated that we must have confidence in ourselves and our endeavors in spite of our current state. He said that we must do what we can do, more than what we want to do, and we must do it now. He did say that we do have the ability, the will and the history of achieving that which lies before us as a nation and as a people. He set the course of his message with, "On this day, we gather because we have chosen hope over fear."

I look forward to the coming weeks and months as our new government begins its journey to wherever it will take us. Today the country is full of hope and promise. I wish I could bottle this optimism and send a morsel to each of my prospects and customers. For it is this promise of our tomorrow that pulls us forward, not the reality of today.

Our new president asked each of us to pick up our arms and prepare to fight. He is not asking us to go to Iraq or Afghanistan. He is not asking us to carry a rifle or similar weapon. He is asking us to continue to do what we do—to use our minds and our skills—but to do it with confidence that it is the right thing to do. His exact words were: "Our minds are no less inventive, our goods and services no less needed than they were last week or last month or last year. Our capacity remains undiminished. But our time of standing pat, of protecting narrow interests and putting off unpleasant decisions — that time has surely passed. Starting today, we must pick ourselves up, dust ourselves off, and begin again the work of remaking America."

It really is "we the people" who will make this happen. We have a president who is a charismatic leader, and he will certainly enroll us into a vision of tomorrow. But make no mistake about it, it will be you and me and many others that make it happen in the end. The timeline will depend upon how quickly we reach a critical mass of those who believe more in the future than the reality of today. While optimism is high, while hope is strong, and while change is in the forefront of everyone's mind, let us not "stand pat." The inauguration of our new president we saw today is as good as any other reason and better than many for us to feel confident enough about what lies ahead to move forward.

In the cold, hard light of day …

*"In day-to-day commerce, television is not so much interested in
the business of communications as in the business of delivering
audiences to advertisers. People are the merchandise, not the
shows. The shows are merely the bait."*

— Les Brown

This morning on my way to work I was thinking about what to write in
this column. Much of what I espouse here comes to me in flashes while
I am doing something else. When I try to remember my brilliance
completely, I find the thoughts that previously excited me often have
faded like a dream, becoming too illusive to remember.

The experience reminds me of when I used to leave a notepad next
to my bed, so that when I woke from a creative dream I could jot down
notes; then, in the morning I would have access to those great ideas
that had come to me in the night. I am sure this process is what led
someone to coin the term "in the cold, hard light of day," because in
the morning, "in the cold, hard light of day," the brilliance written on
my note paper looked like it was penned by someone from an alternate
universe with an entirely different communication medium.

But during my drive this morning I was able to focus on my flash
of brilliance before it faded into unreliable fragments. Now I have the
much easier task of sharing my thoughts with you in such a manner
that you too may be awed by its importance as well as its simplicity.
The topic that excited me so much is improving the effectiveness of
your advertising message. But just stating that improving what you
say to prospective customers offers the best leverage for profits is not

enough to drive the point home, nor is it enough to even hope that you will remember. So, I will give you an analogy.

I have three siblings. Mom wanted a girl so badly, but for her first two pregnancies she was rewarded with two boys, me and brother, Mike. She waited several years and tried one more time for a girl and had identical twin boys. Mom, of course, decided not to tempt fate again. I am the oldest, and ironically, I see my youngest brother most frequently. Greg is younger than Doug, his twin brother, by 33 minutes.

Greg and I live about 15 miles apart, play golf each week, and additionally talk to each other at least that often.

As of late, Greg is obsessed with gas prices. Every phone call begins with him asking how much I paid per gallon for gasoline this week. He is always ready with the location of the least-expensive gasoline in a 30-mile radius. He then proceeds to tell me how buying cheap gas is saving him all sorts of money. He invariably saves 3 to 7 cents more per gallon than I do.

Greg drives an SUV. It is a Mitsubishi that he has had for several years, and he seldom changes the oil and has never tuned-up the engine. Consumer Reports says his SUV should get 18 to 21 miles per gallon, yet Greg only gets 15 miles per gallon. I tell him that if he would get his engine tuned-up he'd save more money on transportation than what he saves from buying the cheapest gas. You see, improving mileage from 15 to 20 miles per gallon offers a 33 percent increase in efficiency. Saving 7 cents on $1.97-per-gallon gasoline only gives 3.5 percent increase in efficiency. By focusing on being cheap, rather than spending a few dollars to make his engine more effective, Greg is losing money.

Greg is like nearly every advertiser I meet. To a person most advertisers believe that getting a lower advertising rate means getting more efficiency, when in fact, spending some money improving their ads through copy testing, professional copywriting or better-quality images, could increase profits to a greater degree than reducing media costs. Brother Greg runs the risk of getting poor-quality gasoline and/ or service when the price of gasoline is his only parameter. And he totally misses the bigger opportunity of increasing mileage, lowering transportation costs, and still being able to enjoy a price advantage when it is available.

For Greg, his cost of transportation involves factors beyond just the cost of gasoline. After explaining it, that has become obvious. But for many advertisers the path to profitability is still as obscure as saving money by improving his vehicle was for Greg. For some reason the results of poor marketing strategies over the years have been blamed on media. New advertisers continue to blame the messenger because that is what those before them have done. And if poor results are only the fault of the media, it exonerates the advertiser of any responsibility for what their message communicates. Rather than fix what is wrong, it drives new advertisers to seek different media and to try different things, at best. At worst it frustrates them to the point of not believing in the value of advertising at all.

Advertisers need to understand this: Testing offers, testing the copywriting, testing ad layouts, improving communication strategies, selling benefits, adding product features, offering warrantees and guarantees—all of these things impact the price-value equation for the buyer. These are but a few of the things that influence the customer's decision to buy. Yet, often the price of the media or the number of people reached is the only criteria advertisers use to judge advertising effectiveness.

Let me share one more analogy. Testing copy on yourself is like taking out your own appendix. It might start out well, but it certainly won't end up as well as you had hoped. When you are working to improve the results of your advertising, spend a little money and make sure the feedback comes from the single expert that counts the most, your target audience. You know too much about your product, and your buying motivations are nothing like those of your prospective customers. You cannot forget enough of what you know about your product to find the objectivity needed here.

When you find salespeople, like mine, who are trained to help you improve your advertising, or when you find a company, who is willing to underwrite a portion of the media expense to improve your advertising, open your checkbook and spend the money. It will be one of the best investments you can make to gaining knowledge about how to make your advertising work on an ongoing basis.

I just shared one of the best tactics for maximizing your advertising spending that I have ever offered. And now I have done it in a way that I've been told gets the message to you in the best possible way. First, I told you what I was going to tell you. Then I told you. And now I am telling you that improving your advertising copy is the highest leverage you can achieve in maximizing profits through effective advertising.

Brother Greg doesn't share my opinion of my brilliance. Because I love him, and I am 11 years his senior, I pretty much feel obligated to give him the benefit of my experience and accumulated knowledge at a moment's notice. Not sharing my view of me, he listens to me sometimes, tolerates me many times, and occasionally tells me what to do with my opinion when I finally do cross the line. That is sad, for it is more important to me that he benefits from my advice than those who read my ADvice for purely entertainment purposes.

"I know what people want …,"

"The fact must never be forgotten that no magazine publisher in the United States could give what it is giving to the reader each month if it were not for the revenue which the advertiser brings the magazine. It is the growth of advertising in this country which, more than any single element, has brought the American magazine to its present enviable position in points of literary, illustrative and mechanical excellence. The American advertiser has made the superior American magazine of today possible"

— Edward Bok

The quiet is deafening, and there is a slight musty odor as you look around the room. The huge walnut table that sits in the center is imposing. High-backed, leather-covered executive chairs flank both sides, and all of them are covered with a layer of dust. Electric cords and local area network cables snake up through the center of table and spiral outward to the work areas in front of each chair. Long ago disconnected, the power is shut off, and the network leads to no one.

This was once a busy, noisy conference room where high-level executives argued the pros and cons of each product offering the company would deliver to its customers. Now it is merely an empty room on the fifth floor of another empty corporate office building. It is not all that different from the hundreds of similar conference rooms and office buildings once used for the same purpose. Like dinosaurs, these rooms no longer survive in a world that has evolved faster than its former occupants.

Not many months earlier the building was full of people who worked for the company. The parking lot was full each day with new-model cars, vans and SUVs. Every night a dozen of so would remain as the owners worked late in the few offices where the lights stayed on until the early hours. There always seemed to be someone inhabiting the building no matter what time of day or night. As morning approached, the tide of employees would again begin to flow into the parking lot and then onto the office building.

Selling products to consumers required lots of people and effort. After 20 years in business, the company head count had grown to several hundred. The company's humble beginnings emerged as two consumers complained that companies were not listening to what they and other consumers wanted. Tired of trying to find the product features that they needed, the two spoke with hundreds of other consumers and created a series of products that nearly sold themselves. Success was too modest of a term for the growth and acclaim achieved by the entrepreneurs and their fledgling company. The founders were tuned in to the market's desires, and they were named industry leaders over night.

Recently, sales were not as robust as in previous years. The selection of products and line extensions that initially brought the company success lost market share, and sales had dwindled to a break-even point. Product-development efforts proved expensive. New line after new line was tested. The results were tepid at best and downright depressing at worst.

Meeting after meeting was held to develop new lines of products. The two founders personally took part in each and every meeting. Ideas were thrown about and always one or both founders would remind those in the room of their past success with the admonition of "I know what people want …"

Across town in a small office were two young businesspeople who met because of their complaints about the first company's product line. Frustrated with poor attempts by the businesses to deliver a product that filled their needs, the two had decided to do it themselves. After dozens of interviews with other frustrated consumers, the two had developed a business plan to market a product design that was the result of hundreds of hours of asking the market what it wanted. The new line was different from what each had initially thought would work, but it was the result of what hundreds of others had said the product line needed to be. So here existed another tuned-in company.

The process of tuning in to the market, as done by the founders of the first company, led them to create a product line that filled a void that was obvious only to the consumers in that market. The resultant success led the founders to believe it was them, and not the process of tuning in to what the consumers wanted, that were responsible for their good fortune. They would have been better served if someone in one of those in the failed product-development meetings had said, "Your opinion, although interesting, is irrelevant …, especially in light of the opinion of those whose problems we wish to solve with the product."

Sometimes the very success we strive so hard to achieve creates in us the condition that leads to our decline. Such as interpreting reasons for product success described in the book Tuned In: *Uncover the Extraordinary Opportunities That Lead to Business Breakthroughs* by Craig Stull, Phil Myers and David Meerman Scott. This book requires many executives to set aside their egos as it uncovers a process anyone can use to develop winning products that resonate with consumer needs and desires. Too many boardrooms echo with "I know what people want …," when in fact, the very act of being in the boardroom disqualifies nearly everyone there from being able to accurately discern what solution consumers are seeking from products.

The assertions of the tuned-in process are supported by examples and a logic that is hard to refute. Many overnight successes are not as they seem. They are not overnight. They are the result of asking hundreds of consumers what they want and then developing a product which provides the solution to their problems.

Current customers are not those who are searching for a new solution, as they will view any new solution as version of your current offering. Those who have no desire for your product now offer the largest growth potential for new products.

In the tuned-in process any product suggestions that are not supported by consumer research should be viewed as interesting opinions. The thoughts, needs and desires of only those laying down cash for your product should be considered. The stronger belief a non-consumer holds about how they "know" what a consumer wants and/ or needs, the farther they are from understanding the market. It is hard for an executive to walk in a consumer's shoes, and it is literally impossible to do so, sitting inside a corporate office.

And before you think to yourself that you are the exception, that you are the one person objective enough to know more than your customers, consider just for a moment that, "Your opinion, although interesting, is irrelevant."

Improving sales when times are tough

"Success is a lousy teacher. It seduces smart people into thinking they can't lose."

— Bill Gates

There are times when sales come easily, and times when they do not. Whatever the reasons, the results need to be the same. You will always have bills to pay. Obligations for the most part do not vary when there is a downturn in the economy or in your particular business segment. As I tell my salespeople, you cannot let the variables determine your results; therefore, it must be your effort. You must work a little bit harder to win dollars that not long ago seemed to flow in without much effort.

Tom Peters, of In Search of Excellence fame, writes in his 1987 book Thriving on Chaos in the chapter titled Launch a Customer Revolution, "No department, including legal and accounting, should exist to protect the firm." In a customer revolution, every department is customer-oriented. And with specific insight he re-defines profit by looking at it from inside total customer satisfaction: "Long-term profit equals revenue from continuously happy customer relationships minus cost." Continuously happy customer relationships are a performance goal that leads to profit; this outlook changes some of the typical business moves made when things get tight.

Also from Thriving on Chaos are these words from Domino Pizza's Phil Bressler, addressing other franchisees: "Sales building is the way to profitability. You can only cut your costs so low before they hurt the customer. You can never raise your sales too high." Advice for building sales profitability comes from delivering more value to more customers rather than the traditional business model of cutting costs to deliver the product less expensively, or to deliver less product in order to enhance margins.

When you think about it, adding product value while others are cutting services and quality is not only a solid business move, it virtually ensures an increase in market share when the market regains its health. Peters suggests doubling the sales force during down periods to increase sales pressure and customer service above and beyond the competition.

Another thought to consider is this. When times are good and sales are brisk, there occurs an atmosphere of being too busy to build and develop new markets. The arrogance of easy sales leads companies to be less customer-focused because sales are not won through hard-fought battles.

Typically, companies design themselves to achieve economies with employees giving 100 percent effort. When this occurs, where is the room for growth? Where are the energy and resource reserves that could be used to take the production and revenues to the next level? Certainly it will not be done by new employees that need to be trained to participate in a productivity explosion.

Most often companies do just the opposite. They cut capacity by cutting labor. Lowell Mayone vice president of Hallmark in 1987 says, "If we have too many people, we consider it a management problem, not an employee problem." In truth, management is responsible for developing plans and products to utilize available labor. A failure to allocate labor resources and generate a profit is indeed failure of management.

When the going gets tough, the tough get going. Well maybe. I would say that when the going gets tough, you severely test your customer relationships. More often than not, consumers and businesses alike cut back expenditures during tough times, based upon perceived need more than real need. Solid customer relationships can ensure a bridge across times of economic uncertainty.

How do you differentiate yourself from the rest? Market, advertise and serve your customer more and better than ever before. Studies of recessionary periods back through the 1960s show that companies that invest in advertising and marketing during uncertain economic periods show increased market share and vitality after the economy improves.

Of those who do cut back their initiatives to communicate product value to customers, only a fraction, survive long-term.

Who is the judge of quality? I mean, who knows if I am turning out a quality product or not? My years of experience must mean that I know something, so I should know about the quality of my own work—right? If I don't, then what is the value of all these years? Well, the only judge of quality is in the eye of the customer. Regardless of what we think, perceive or know, the customer's judgment with their purchasing dollar is the decision that will seal our fate. Listen to your customer. Listen like your very life depended upon it. Don't listen to confirm that you are right; listen to find out where you are wrong, and then have the courage to change it. Unless you are spending only your own money to keep your company afloat, your opinion is the last one you want to hear.

The same goes for value-added and product differentiation. Listen to your customer to find out what is important and what makes you different. You will most likely be surprised at what you learn. Keep asking the same questions over and over of different customers. You will find that these things change over time with the ebb and flow of your customer base, as well as when their needs evolve and change. Your experience may stem from many years in the past, but you need to know what specific needs are as of now. Forget all that you know and attack the problem to learn everything anew. Expect things to be different, but allow yourself to be surprised if some turn out to be the same.

Making leaps in generating results seldom happens from "doing more of the same." Great strides in performance usually result from doing things differently rather than doing more of a familiar process. Reinventing how you do things is hard when you have achieved moderate success with your current structure. Most people don't like change. Even fewer want to change processes that have led to a current level of success. Our human nature tells us that it is better to continue the moderate success with which we are familiar than to take a risk with a new procedure to possibly achieve a larger success we have never seen.

Generating increased sales in rough times takes courage. It requires you to question things that have worked in the past. Some of those things that need to be questioned are so ingrained that most of the time we don't even see them. It is a good exercise to have a friend, who is not associated with your business, sit down with you. You should explain to them just how your business works. As you explain the various facets of your job, allow them ask you why—over and over and over. Eventually, you will begin to see through some of the assumptions you have made and taken as facts. Then you will be empowered to look at the type of changes that can get you beyond doing the same old thing just a little bit better.

Far too often new competitors enter our business categories and revolutionize how we do business. The reason they can do so, is because they aren't smart enough to know it can't be done that way. We too, must practice being ignorant of our industry. It may be the only way we can adequately reward ourselves for all the years we have spent doing our job. Being able to suspend our self-imposed limitations and still use our specific knowledge is not at all easy. But it could be the genius that leads us to take everything to the next level. The first thing to understand is that the best time to grow is when others are not.

The healing power of crafts

"Far better it is to dare mighty things, to win glorious triumphs, even though checkered by failure, than to take rank with those poor spirits who neither enjoy much nor suffer much, because they live in the gray twilight that knows not victory nor defeat."

— Theodore Roosevelt

The other day I heard a quote that struck me as profound. I apologize for not being able to credit its source, nor to be able to do more than offer my paraphrased version. My memory of it is, "Isn't it interesting that human beings, who enter and exit this world in very solitary ways, spend almost every moment in between attempting to connect with as many other human beings as possible."

The statement strikes me as being very true, and the wise advertiser should always keep in mind the human need to interact meaningfully with others. If all advertisers understood and used this universal need to connect with and to be acknowledged by other human beings in their advertising, surely we'd all be more successful.

Crafters are by nature some of the most compassionate and generous people in the world. Within days after Hurricane Katrina hit the Big Easy, quilters rallied and sent semi-truck load after semi truck load of quilts to the victims. Similarly, crocheters and knitters send infant caps to Third-World nations for newborn babies. The knitting guild and crochet guild regularly make afghans for the homeless and needy. Each natural disaster provides ample motivation for generous crafters to ply their skills and benefit those whose lives have been affected by adversity.

Who benefits the most? Granted those who receive handmade items to protect and keep them warm are blessed, but what about the giving folks who made them? Routinely, companies survey magazine and book readers about their crafting habits. Almost every survey shows that crafting in order to give the items to the needy is nearly the top motivation. Do crafters do this purely because they are selfless? No. The process of making and giving items is not only cathartic, but it provides to many a sense of control during periods of chaos. So whether it is due to natural disasters or economic uncertainty, crafting gives an individual the peace of mind that he or she is gaining control over a small area and doing something fight back.

One of life's biggest desires is to want to make a difference in the world. There will always be room for businesses that facilitate the basic human need. Many folks avoid or resist direct pleas for their help, but hundreds of thousands still want to make a difference. Even more want to do something that allows them to feel as if they are exerting control over what feels to be an uncontrollable environment.

Successful craft retailers organize classes, sessions or campaigns for customers to contribute to those less fortunate. Others entice crafters to be generous by becoming a collection point for crafts to then send to the less fortunate affected by recent floods and weather-related tragedies. Appealing to the consumer's higher motives is not just a good business strategy; it also surrounds the retailer with an image of generosity too.

More importantly, a retailer who trains his consumers to be generous and caring ensures additional sales without relying on the usual self-serving "buy now" banter. It is good business and being a good neighbor to carry and communicate the message of giving. Consumers are empowered when given the opportunity to make a difference in the lives of those in need.

Many times we have viewed scenes from areas ravaged by floods, tornados or other natural disasters showing homeowners who have lost their homes and belongings. Many are torn and wounded by such unforeseen tragedies. In our own way each of us wants to reach out and help. Only by the grace of God have we avoided facing the same plight.

Reaching out to those in need helps us cope as much as our contribution bolsters those whose sense of hope has been shaken to it core by Mother Nature's fury. These moments of difficulty get in our faces to remind us of our inevitable solitary natures. It makes us work even harder at connecting with others, so we avoid what that absolute solitude represents.

In a summer of turmoil we should encourage others to reach out. Not just as a good business practice, but so that we may all genuinely connect with others in meaningful ways. If crafters do indeed make many of their craft items to give away, maybe they have discovered the real nature of crafting. As with life, maybe its purpose is to help us relate to others and build community in an uncertain world.

What's the use ...?

"Next to Christianity, advertising is the greatest force in the world. And I say that without sacrilege or disrespect. Advertising makes people discontented. It makes them want things they don't have. Without discontent, there is no progress, no achievement."

— Ray Locke

I thought it was just me. Then I broached the topic to a couple of people in my department, as well as a few others I deal with regularly, and I got the exact same response. As I talked to more associates I encountered the same apathy at every corner. When I finally spoke the words, the answer was nearly universal: "What's the use?"

In my department, my industry, and even in my hometown at some level, there seems to be a universal frustration with the current state of affairs, coupled with apathy about putting forth any effort to change things. The passion that used to lie just under the surface for so many now appears to be replaced by a sense of hopelessness. I don't know what is causing it exactly. It may be the fault of the news media, reporting negative story after negative story. It might be the slowing in certain economic sectors that is dimming people's sense of hope. Or maybe everyone is just tired of fighting what appears as a losing battle.

Come to think of it, I run into resignation quite a bit. Many advertisers face the frustration of the marketplace by disengaging from commerce and observing it as if they were watching from the sidelines. They watch with detachment, as if the fact that their company is getting pounded by the competition is someone else's problem and not their own. When trying to get them to engage in the game, the "What's the use" look comes over their face.

During this time of year, facing resignation like this is even more of a challenge for me. March is a wonderful time for me as a basketball fan. In mid-March the NCAA tournament begins my dream weekend of 49 basketball games over a period of 96 hours. The next weekend is only slightly less exciting with 12 games in 96 hours. And the championship weekend is limited to just 3 games in 48 hours, but they are big games. There are 64 must-win games in 19 days. Could it get any better? For the 65 teams and approximately 750 student athletes, it is a special time. Hope flows eternal. There is always an underdog that steals everyone's heart. Davidson University was this year's dark horse, and they did not disappoint anyone.

Saturday April 5, the afternoon of the final-four weekend, CBS sports began their pre-game coverage with a documentary I am sure too few people got to see. A 13-year-old boy from Arizona named Austin Guttwein showed how it is possible for one person to change the world. When he was 9, Austin heard about children in Zambia being orphaned at a horrendous rate because of the large number of adults in Zambia dying of AIDS.

Austin organized Hoops of Hope where children raised money through pledges for shooting free throws. In 2006 Austin's goal was to raise money for education so the orphaned children of Zambia could learn. He got his friends to gather pledges against their efforts to shoot free throws. The idea caught on and grew past Austin's community. Several events were staged, and as you will read on their Web site, through Austin's efforts Hoops of Hope participants raised $85,000 in 2006 to help build the Johnathan Sim Legacy School in Twatchiyanda, Zambia. In 2007, the ante was upped and Austin's Hoops of hope exceeded their goal, raising over $200,000. They used $150,000 to build a medical testing lab and voluntary counseling center in Sinazongwe, Zambia. The additional funds went to the school and other programs.

The documentary pointed out how Austin had achieved extraordinary results while remaining a very typical young person -- a pretty much ordinary person doing extraordinary things. Austin had a passion to make a difference. He did not concern himself with his age, the enormity of the task, or even if his efforts would be enough. He optimistically followed his passion and made a great difference.

Edmund Burke, the English philosopher said, "The only thing necessary for the triumph of evil is for good men to do nothing." I guess Burke's quote could be paraphrased to say, "All that is necessary to kill someone's optimism is to lure them into thinking, 'what's the use of trying?'"

Inspiring articles, movies, or even speeches at times, are sometimes all we have to hold on to when we are in the midst of battle and do not yet have the end in sight. Those inches or seconds before our victories are often the very darkest moments, those times when our resolve is at its lowest ebb. We need inspiration to compel us to remember the depth of our commitment and to see things through to completion.

It is always worthwhile to make the effort. The act of attempting the impossible challenges the very limits of our knowledge and understanding. Those who have done so have been almost universally ridiculed prior to their acclaim. And the bigger the victory, the more foolish they looked at the start. Stories of heroes and heroines do not begin with fame. They begin with trial. They begin with frustration. And, yes, they begin with resignation.

When the populace believes hope is gone, the opportunity is created for great deeds --accomplishments achieved by ordinary people who, in the face of apathy, become committed to completing that which others have abandoned. Those people are acknowledged as remarkable. Austin Guttwein's father is amazed at how his remarkable son is just an ordinary kid. And the truth be known, most of our other heroes are mere mortals too. They just don't buy into "what is the use?" Instead, they say, "Why not?"

Sale -- Market Share 50% Off

"Advertising is criticized on the ground that it can manipulate consumers to follow the will of the advertiser. The weight of evidence denies this ability. Instead, evidence supports the position that advertising, to be successful, must understand or anticipate basic human needs and wants and interpret available goods and services in terms of their want-satisfying abilities. This is the very opposite of manipulation."

— Charles H. Sandage

In their newly released book, The Three Laws of Performance: Rewriting the Future of Your Organization and Your Life, published by Jossey-Bass, the authors Steve Zaffron and Dave Logan assert that people react perfectly to their interpretation of events. People's actions are congruent with how the world occurs to them. Helping them to interpret what occurs for them in a new and empowering way is the key to changing, and more importantly, improving performance.

Sometimes the obvious and most direct solution is the hardest one to accept. If that were not true, there would be virtually no response to the get-rich-quick schemes and scams that abound all around us, especially in times like now of economic stress and of great change.

Most everyone knows that Warren Buffet is an American investor, businessman and philanthropist. He is one of the world's most successful investors, and the largest shareholder and CEO of Berkshire Hathaway. One of his guidelines for investors is to "buy fear and sell greed." What he means Is to buy when the vast majority is fearful of the future and thus selling their investments. This is the best time to buy at bargain prices. He also suggests selling investments when confidence is high and everyone's demand of buying is driving the prices to higher points.

I cannot imagine many who would not want the financial success that Mr. Buffet has worked so hard to enjoy. In times of less economic extremes, being able to judge the "fear," and the "greed," mentioned by Mr. Buffet is more of an art because it is not as obvious as now. But now, the fear is so prevalent that in spite of what is in front of us, most are running with the herd. Even those in a position to take advantage of bargains in the stock market are selling.

Seeing the stock market as an opportunity right now indeed takes a new and empowering interpretation of current events. Just as it does for businesses in our crafting industry to see that we are in the midst of a market-share sale. A great portion of the companies in our industry are pulling back their investments into their own success and market share, choosing instead to reserve cash. We all know that during times of economic crisis that our industry seems to do OK because people have more of a tendency to cocoon and do entertaining and less-expensive things at home. Crafting easily fills that need.

Yet the fear in other markets is causing companies in ours to step back and react as if things are really bad. From the reports we have seen, things are not all that bad. My company in many areas is doing very well this year. And, in fact, many of those we deal with are doing much better than most would suspect.

So why is everyone acting as if it is worse than it is? Maybe we don't want to be irresponsible and get caught by surprise by some impending economic doom. As Zaffron and Logan would say, we are acting congruent with how things are occurring to us. We are reacting perfectly to the interpretation of events that says the economy has slowed. But what if our interpretation of the economy in general is incorrect in our specific and targeted market? Opportunities may not be seen as such. We may not only view the glass as half empty, we may also believe that nobody wants the water.

People tend to make more decisions based upon emotions than they make based upon logic. During times of stress many of us become like an exposed nerve irritated at the very presence of anything that threatens our view of the future. But even Warren Buffet's logic of buying fear and selling greed is not enough for us to take advantage what might lie before us.

In the meantime, companies that have built market share are cutting back on their marketing efforts and are not adequately defending what they spent so much to attain. Market share in many categories is available for the investment of pennies compared to the dollars you might have to invest in a stronger economic time to actually compete.

There are stories of many companies that exist today who stole market share in previous economic slowdowns. Their critics call them lucky. But those who fought the battle will tell you that they bought their market share when it was on sale. It was on sale when their competitors thought cash was more important than prosperity.

Zaffron and Logan would say to look at yourself and your company a year or so down the road in a dominant position in your market, enjoying the benefits of everyone knowing you and being the first option that comes to mind. If in fact that is where you will be then, what steps must you take now to get there? Wouldn't you rather buy that market share now for 50 cents on the dollar rather than when things are strong and you may have to spend a dollar and 25 cents against the dollar for that type of growth?

Our economy will improve. Of that we are certain. How long it will take, we do not know. But if history has taught us much, it should have taught us that the difference between winning and losing may be only one or two decisions. Those decisions may rest solely on our interpretation of the glass being half empty or the glass being half full. Can we afford not to invest in our future when many seem to be running away from it?

Things we do to ourselves

"We grew up founding our dreams on the infinite promise of American advertising. I still believe that one can learn to play the piano by mail and that mud will give you a perfect complexion."

— Zelda Fitzgerald

It is that time of year again. Most of us are still doing the autopsy on last year while putting the finishing touches on plans and forecasts for the current year. If you are like me, no matter how well last year went, it is still not good enough. And next year's goal already seems daunting. It causes me to think about human nature and the quirks in each of us that contribute to our frustrating results.

Over the years, I have sold many forms of advertising. Some of it was easy to sell, and some of it was hard to sell. Always, the product was essentially the same. I was selling access to a specific audience who had the ability to increase product sales for my customers. The less specific I was about my product's characteristics, the more it seemed to be viewed as a commodity.

I have spent 31 years doing what I do. That's not a complete lifetime, but it certainly is enough to have gathered a significant volume of evidence that supports some of my theories sufficiently for me to view those theories as fact. One of those evidence-supported theories is that an advertised product holds more value in the eyes of the market than an unadvertised product. Too many companies incorrectly believe that their brand is known far and wide, when in fact the opposite is closer to the truth.

With all due respect to all of the media companies where I have worked, media seems to be as bad an offender of this as anyone. Broadcast and print media have as bad a track record of advertising their brands as any other company out there. This is simply another case of the shoemaker's son going barefoot. Beyond my evidence, it is also common sense that advertised brands rank higher in value in the minds of consumers. After all, don't we value the familiar more than something we know nothing about?

Unless the advertising message positions the product as affordable or economical, the more pervasive the advertising message, the higher the perceived value of the product. Most products do, however, inadvertently limit their value equation by comparison to other products, or by a specific appeal to an economic market segment. In the absence of these factors, additional advertising expenditures do increase the intrinsic value of the product.

In every study I have seen over a 31-year career, advertised products comfortably outsell unadvertised products every time. There are no ties or even close calls. Hands down, advertised beats unadvertised. Yet each year, there are companies who believe that by cutting advertising they can finally get where they want to go. There are always new businesses going up against giants in their category, believing they can do so without promoting their product.

Another theory is not mine, but I have gathered more than a little bit of evidence in its defense. The theory is this: Doing the same thing over and over is bound to generate the same result. To be honest, outside influences on a repeated process do affect the outcome, but only minimally. It really is insane how companies continue flawed processes because they are familiar, yet expect the current version will generate a totally new and desired result. Change in the business world is actually far rarer than most people would believe. While definitions and descriptions change, the essential processes have a way of remaining the same, and unfortunately, so do the repeated unacceptable results.

Change that is true change is not embraced by much of anyone. The human mind and business mindset scream for a predictable order to the chaos of the free marketplace. In our desire for a simplified understanding, we often take flawed processes and just rename them or rework them without changing the recognizable mechanics that generate the results and that make us feel comfortable. Better the failure we know than the discomfort we do not know. Nothing troubles businesspeople more than throwing everything out the window and starting all over. This causes so much stress that against all common sense human beings will actually repeat failed processes in order to avoid the unknown, which has a greater chance of success.

One way to begin to embrace change is to focus on the learning aspect rather than what is different. Continually ask yourself, "What is the lesson that this experience is teaching me?" By focusing on learning, you accept that you do not know what the outcome will be. This removes the fear of failure and unleashes a powerful curiosity which fuels progress.

Individuals often validate themselves and identify strongly with their accomplishments. In doing so, they prevent themselves from being able to learn more. The reasoning that hampers learning is, "If I have invested so much time and effort into becoming who I am, then I should know everything of importance in my area of expertise. Therefore, if it is something I do not know, either it must not be worthwhile to know it, or my value is not as much as I thought." Needless to say, learning something new at the expense of someone's self-evaluation is likely not to happen voluntarily.

It is a foible of human nature that the very thing we desire the most is often the most evasive thing for us to achieve. I only need to look at my scales each morning for the truth in this statement. Being successful in business is hardly ever the result of attempting to be successful. Those who focus on success think it is the shortest distance to their goal. But in the real world it often is the road to the very opposite. Highly successful people will tell you that success is the by-product of more lofty pursuits. If you are attempting to be the best in customer service, you may well fall short of that goal. But in that pursuit you may become very successful financially and professionally, depending upon how diligently you apply your efforts.

You can witness this in the efforts of some companies whose only goal is to make money. Invariably, these companies are never satisfied with their results. But when the goal is to serve customers, benefit mankind, nurture and empower their employees within the structure of a profit-making entity, the outcome is often amazing. What is the reason? It's easy; the most common and basic human need is to make a difference in the world and impact the lives of others. Making money, unless you are a Warren Buffet, is one of the most forgettable achievements a person can accomplish. Just one dollar more erases your previous record. When the money is spent, there is a need to repeat your "success" or be replaced as the latest hero.

I train salespeople to be better at achieving results for their clients than anyone else. What do I get for that goal: record sales results every year, satisfied employees who understand how to and have the desire to make a difference with their customers, and an increasingly larger group of loyal customers. My salespeople make extraordinary incomes, not because money is their goal, but because they make a difference in the lives of others. And they seldom grow tired of the effort, because making a difference for others is more rewarding than just making money. We don't start our day by asking, "How can we cut our expenses to increase our profits?" We start by asking, "How we can improve our customers' businesses, and hence, their lives?" Yes, we do have a profit responsibility, but that is not enough to inspire performance where nine out of 10 people say no. Our goal is far beyond just making money. And that is our advantage.

2008 will be another year of challenges. We will win some great victories and lose some close battles. We will, or we will not achieve our sales forecast. But for my staff, we will be smarter because we always try to learn, so we have something new to share. We will genuinely endeavor to improve the businesses of those clients who place their trust in us. For sure, we will carry the banner that advertising works, as I have personally witnessed for the last 31 years. Next year as we review, we will again wish for higher results, possibly fear the daunting future ahead, and even wonder what human traits will step in our way as we embark on 2009.

It is about time we all grew up

"Decision is a sharp knife that cuts clean and straight; indecision is a dull one that hacks and tears and leaves ragged edges behind it."

— Gordon Graham

Becoming upset is the result of unfulfilled expectations, thwarted actions or stifled intentions. We go along in life with pictures in our mind about many things. When a reality occurs that does not fit our vision of what things should look like, we are torn between what we want and what is so. The difference causes us to become upset. I, like others I know, probably spend too much time in the world of "should-be," a place where I can project my expectations upon the screen and make others wrong because the reality they created failed to live up to my vision.

Such a thing happened two weeks ago. The house I live in is approaching 30 years old, and as such, is beginning to show wear and tear. If I were single and living alone, I would move to a newer home in town. But my wife, who has more emotion invested in where we live, not only likes our older home but loves our neighborhood too. So, I am left to do the repairs myself or find suitable tradesmen to repair the failings of my maturing home.

To locate a craftsman I scanned the local newspaper for ads of those ready to serve incompetent handymen like me. Our small-town paper had no less than nine such ads suggesting that hapless homeowners just call to arrange for a free estimate and the solution to their woes. I tore out the page and picked up the telephone. Twenty minutes later I had called them all, left five messages on answering machines, and was certain that at least one or two callbacks would happen within an hour or so. None came that night. The next evening I called the five numbers with answering machines again and left nearly the exact same message: I needed someone to do work for me, and I wanted to talk about hiring them.

Please understand, the ads in the newspaper were for very specific types of remodeling services, and I only called those that fit my needs exactly. I did not call a painter asking for a roofing quote. At the end of the second evening, I was no closer to solving my problem than I was when I first picked up our local newspaper.

I waited an entire week, expecting one of the five tradesmen to call me back, but no one called. I thought long and hard over the weekend about tackling the repair work myself. But as I mentioned, I am challenged when it comes to certain types of home repair. With certain power tools I resemble a characters from Texas Chainsaw Massacre more than a home owner. So I called the five again on Monday evening. This time I reached a live person on the fourth call who told me that he really did not do the two items that I called for, but were listed in his ad as his specialty. The fifth number I left another message, and he called me back later that evening. He apologized that he had not returned my two calls from the previous week, and then told me he was booked for the next two months and could not help me.

The next evening, my fourth night of trying to spend money with people who have put an ad in the paper saying that they could solve my problem, I caught another live person on my second call. Let me insert here that these nine ads—the four with answering machines, the four who did not answer their telephone nor have machines, and the one who advertises services he doesn't perform—run every day in my local paper. Finally, someone called who was interested in talking to me, but (remember he called me) he asked me to call him back in about five minutes after he found a pen and paper to write down my name, address and number. I called him back, probably a little too soon, because it took him seven rings before he picked up the phone. He told me he only did quotes in the evening after he has finished his efforts of the day on the jobs he is currently doing. So he took my information and told me he'd call the next week on the day he could come by to see me. He was not sure, but it would be no more than a week.

Since 1975 I have been involved in the selling advertising in one form or the other. People who own small businesses are always telling me that advertising does not work. In my own town I found nine small businesspeople, none of whom understand that in most cases you only get one chance to impress a new customer. Every one of those nine blew the opportunity to set themselves apart in my eyes. I now know that none of them are very good at customer service, something that I will leverage when it comes time to getting the best price.

Am I upset? As a consumer, yes I am. I longed to be treated as a welcomed prospect by these businesspeople. But I was put into a position of chasing them down to get just one of them to consider taking my money in return for performing the services that all of them promoted and competed for my attention with their ads. My impression is that none of these tradesmen are very successful, which suggests I will need to monitor their progress on my project. If they handle their remodeling efforts the way they handle their customer service, I might be better to off to do it myself.

Advertising can hurt a business that is not prepared to serve its customers, as much as it can help one that is ready to expand. I tell folks that advertising is like a magnifying glass. It will amplify whatever is there. If it is good, more people will know about it. Unfortunately, if it is bad, the same thing will happen.

Today in 2008 people are starved for personalized attention. Most of us are more than willing to pay premiums for the assurance that what we say is heard, that our desires are being addressed, and that someone is thinking of our wants and needs more than our money. Herein lays a ripe opportunity to make a difference, and all it seems to breed is more indifference.

Why would it take me 24 telephone calls on four different days over an eight-day period to finally get one person to talk to me? Are we all so self-absorbed that we are not listening to others? Is there so much opportunity out there that we need not even concern ourselves with common courtesy and customer service? What would be the opportunity for a company that answered, perhaps not every phone call, but to at least return every phone message the day it was received? I have to believe that the best jobs would go to the company that would at least attempt to be responsive. The problem is that mediocrity is making several segments of the service industry a seller's market. So many are so poor at providing customer service that we accept the first response in many instances for fear nobody else will respond.

We are becoming a society that surrenders to procedures rather than a society in search of an opportunity to serve. It is far easier to put all of the food on the breakfast menu into the trash at 10:30 a.m. at MacDonald's than it is to serve the 10:45 appetite of a customer wanting a late breakfast during the menu transition period.

We are shuffled from automated operator to automated operator on telephone systems rather than being immediately addressed by a live person with common sense, logic and the proper authority to address our needs. Businesses measure how effective they are in minimizing contact with customers rather than seizing the opportunity to engage with customers in order confidently better serve their needs and concerns.

One day the pendulum will swing back in the other direction. Focus on the customer will return. Those companies that embrace their customer relationships will flourish. Their CEO's will be invited to speak to scores of executives who have minimized customer contact and hence sales revenues for many years. Someone will coin a simple new phrase like "the customer is king." It will become a rallying point for a business revolution, millions will be made from seminars, new books will be published, conference halls will be filled to hear the new order of customer service, and life will change until someone decides to push back the pendulum to save their way to prosperity. My only concern will be if I can find someone to install my replacement windows before my house falls down around them.

Change or Progress

"Ethics in advertising? Advertising is about as ethical as the American public. About as ethical as you and your neighbors. About as selfish as you and your acquaintances. It has about the same moral standards as the upper socioeconomic strata of society because it is created, approved and paid for by the upper echelons of modern U.S. society. I'll modify that to say that it is a little more ethical, a little more moral, than the upper economic strata of society. Why? Because advertising lives in a fish bowl. It is the most visible of all commercial practices. It has 200 million critics. And no business, no communications medium, no art form (or whatever you want to call advertising), no other enterprise has so many watchdogs."

— Morris Hite

This morning I had a conference call with a customer. In short, he was upset with what he claims is under-delivery of our audience. It seems that what he expected to be delivered and what my salesperson promised were different. I can understand the frustration he felt when he got something different than what he anticipated. Our conversation escalated to a point that left the description "cordial" somewhere in the rearview mirror. After I hung up from the call, I felt badly about how passionate I became in defending my point of view.

You see, I learned long ago that the "facts," no matter how objectively you think you have considered them, are still a matter of perspective. A multidimensional view of a situation will almost always deliver multiple impressions of what it means. If you look long enough, there is always an interpretation of the current situation that supports your point of view. As much as I believe in my version of truth, my customer has every bit as much the right to do so too.

I also learned that every time someone calls to tell me I have an ugly baby (that is, deliver an opinion about my product that is not as complimentary as the opinion I hold); I have a penchant for zealously defending my understanding of facts. Because I know this about myself, I more often than not postpone conversations that I expect to go this way, hoping that the other party's need to express his or her opinion fades from the requestor's mind.

In my conversation today, we talked about progress our industry is making. My customer was, no doubt, thinking about how I should accommodate his needs by changing my advertising rates to fit his metrics. I, on the other hand, was thinking if my customer would change his metrics to match the evolving cost structure that affects my advertising rates how progressive that would be on his behalf.

This was a classic example of how everyone wants progress, but nobody wants to change. When he is forced to amend his ways, I see progress, but when I am forced to make changes, I see it as unnecessary.

It is true that you either grow, or you wither and die. For in our world nothing remains the same. The environment of business is constantly in a state of evolution—moving, growing and changing in response to all of the forces exerted upon the market; so anything that is not moving in response to those pressures on an equal basis is losing ground.

To change is extremely difficult. As human beings we are willing to do many things to avoid changes, and instead often create just the illusion of change. One of the easiest of these illusions for us to do is to redefine (or rename) familiar things. Many times we substitute new in-vogue language for familiar terms in an equation and believe that we are using a whole new set of metrics.

Another trick we play on ourselves is to add layers and layers of meaningless detail in hopes of making a relatively simply metric seem very complicated and hence harder to accomplish, thus making failure a more reasonable outcome.

I believe in simple metrics. One plus one equals two. Too many variables exponentially expand possible interpretations. Managing as few key metrics as possible increases the leverage you hold over processes.

If you must micromanage multiple metrics to make something viable, you may well be in a mature, declining or over-saturated market that lacks the long-term potential many businesses require.

My customer and I parted ways this morning with me committed to answering his specific concerns, which I anticipate will be a second round of calling my baby ugly. It will be difficult to resist my initial reaction of defending my reality, where each of my products serves the needs of every customer. I spend a large amount of time making sure my products are everything we promise our customers. So, I will need to bite my tongue (maybe until it bleeds) in order to hear his interpretation of the facts as seen through the lens of his glasses.

Sometimes two people aiming at the same thing but coming from different starting places can easily shoot each other rather than the bull's-eye of their common target.

"No thanks, I can do it myself ..."

"Life shrinks or expands in proportion to one's courage."

— Anais Nin

The other day my daughter called and said, "Dad, I have a problem -- can you help me out?" It was not a big thing, and she probably could have found a solution on her own without my involvement had I not answered the phone. But she did two things that were really smart. She made life easier on herself, and she made me feel important. Just by asking for my help she gave me the gift of making a tangible difference in her life right then. And she paid me with the most valuable currency she has, her appreciation.

When I was younger, I must have really been stupid, because the things that I knew as an absolute certainty then are totally wrong now. Take for instance asking for help. Like most people I always viewed asking for help as a weakness. The mere thought of doing so made me shudder. To actually let another human being know that you were incapable of getting something done and finding an answer on your own was a sure indication of your incompetence. And that was something no self-respecting individual would do.

I call it the "Lone Ranger" syndrome. But even the Lone Ranger had the help of Tonto. Most of us tend to refuse the help of others and try to brave our way through situations where we clearly need guidance -- trying to cope all on our own, because we think that's the way competent human beings ought to do things.

Now, I am not talking about a situation like being in a retail store where you are approached by the sales "associate" with a "May, I help you find something?" I have been there plenty of times, and in all honesty,

I am as guilty as anyone with the "I'm just looking ..." line. Face it, it rolls off of your tongue so easily that every salesperson identifies with our discomfort -- that's the reason they back down when they know we don't want to appear clueless, or just don't want to be bothered. Those more-attuned sales personnel have improved their responses smartly to say, "I see you are just looking now. My name is Larry, and I'll be right over here in case you have any questions." It's a great way to provide an opening for service without charging over, grabbing the customer by the lapels, and coercing him or her into buying the day's five sale items. It addresses what everyone knows you are going to say to get rid of the salesperson, and it acknowledges it in an open way while silently saying, "I'm here to do my job to help you if and when you feel you need it."

But that's not the type of help I'm talking about. Think about the people who mean the most in your life, and what help they may need from time to time. It pains me to see someone I care about do something that will cost them time, money and even harm. Yet many of my relatives and loved ones charge forward in areas where they obviously need guidance, need an extra hand or God forbid, the knowledge or experience of another. I will bet you have had that happen in your life too.

There is another side of the situation. It is that certain feeling. That is, the feeling you get when you see that you made a difference in life of someone else. Man, that feeling is the deepest satisfaction I get from my career. Money is fine, but genuine appreciation is like a drug that keeps me returning and returning. When you can offer a hand, make a suggestion, or roll up your sleeves to lighten someone's burden, the look on his or her face afterward is more rewarding than anything.

I work with salespeople. The career of sales is one of the most emotionally challenging jobs there is. It is very solitary. The realities are ruthless. You get absolutely no points for effort. The fine line between success and failure is affected by so many elements that are totally outside the control of anyone, that believing you are in control is an illusion too. When one of the salespeople I work with gets depressed or down, or is having a particularly hard time, I suggest that they go out and help someone without the expectation of anything in return. It's funny, because as the director of a sales department, the first thought they have is that I want them to lull someone into a position where they can sell them something by doing them a favor.

It's not that at all. Helping others gives the biggest reward to you. If you ever get into a philosophical discussion about the search for the meaning of life, you will eventually get to the root of it; it is this: "I want to make a difference." It is the most basic goal the individual has. Every action we take comes from this most basic need. Selflessly helping other people is the shortest route to fulfilling your destiny. That's why I tell a depressed salesperson to go out and help someone -- anyone. It will make the salesperson feel good, and maybe, just maybe, that salesperson will feel good enough about himself or herself that prospects will see a difference in that salesperson. The prospect may come to understand through that salesperson's attitude that selling our product is more about helping the prospect than it is about making money for the sales company. That may sound counter-intuitive; after all, a company is in business to make money. But a company that focuses only on the monetary aspect is missing something that will translate to all of the other individuals with whom they come in contact. From the outside vendors and customers to the internal management and employees, the lack of "soul" will come across and color every transaction. The attitude of helpfulness, and being willing to accept help, sets up a two-way exchange between people that allows them to make that difference in life and to express appreciation. We are all in this together – the truth is, we will all succeed together, or we will all fail.

As I have grown older, I have come to realize what an opportunity I have to make a difference in the lives of others, not by what I do for them, but by allowing them to contribute to me. I've shared this with my daughter and others. She really does understand that asking for my help is a gift that she is giving me. Yes, it makes her life easier. But it serves my need to be of service, and helps fulfill my desire to make a difference while I'm here on planet Earth.

The words "No thanks, I can do it myself," do not come from me as easily now as they did when I was younger, because I know they take away a gift of fulfillment from the person to whom I say them. Understanding how satisfying making a contribution to another human can be, I offer my aid more frequently than in the past. Although it seems strange, when I offer my help now, I cannot help but feel a little selfish, understanding that I will get the deepest satisfaction from my efforts, because so very few people know the gift that they give to me when they say yes.